Advance Praise for
The Collected Schizophrenias

"Necessary and illuminating. In these elegant essays, Esmé Weijun Wang insightfully dissects the many false stories we tell ourselves about mental and physical illness while investigating her own diagnosis of schizoaffective disorder. *The Collected Schizophrenias* is a brilliant guide to the complexities of thinking about illness, and mental illness in particular. It will bring hope to others searching to understand their own diagnoses, and the lyric precision of her writing is a solace and pleasure in its own right."   —Meghan O'Rourke

"*The Collected Schizophrenias* is a masterful braiding of the achingly personal and the incisively researched. With graceful, penetrating intelligence and a strong dose of wit, Esmé Weijun Wang creates a container that can hold the complexities and contradictions of her diagnosis, while addressing the larger issue of how our society marginalizes its mentally ill population. This book is a vital, illuminating window onto the world we all already live in, but find all too easy to ignore."   —Alexandra Kleeman

"Through the wide-angle lens of her own life, Esmé Weijun Wang comprehensively takes in the science, literature, art, institutions, spiritualism, and popular myths of schizophrenia, fashioning a tableau of intense clarity and contrast. You won't find any pity-baiting, sensationalism, or false positivity here; Wang is so candidly *aware* that I'd trust her over my own diary."   —Tony Tulathimutte

"In this remarkable, riveting collection of essays, Esmé Weijun Wang offers us an all-access pass to her beautiful, unquiet mind in what can only be described as an act of profound generosity. Rarely has a book about living with mental illness felt so immediate, raw, and powerful."   —Dani Shapiro

"This mesmerizing collection of essays has achieved the rarest of rarities—a meaningful and expansive language for a subject that has been long bound by both deep revulsion and intense fascination. Brimming with poetry, inquisition, and a big pulsing heart."   —Jenny Zhang

"*The Collected Schizophrenias* is at once generous and brilliantly nuanced, rigorous and bold. It had me rethinking what it is to be well or ill, and what it means to be in a body—to be, that is, alive. A powerful, extraordinary book."   —R. O. Kwon, author of *The Incendiaries*

THE
COLLECTED
SCHIZOPHRENIAS

Also by Esmé Weijun Wang

The Border of Paradise

THE
COLLECTED
SCHIZOPHRENIAS

ESSAYS

ESMÉ WEIJUN WANG

Graywolf Press

Essays in this collection appeared originally in different form in the following publications:
"Toward a Pathology of the Possessed" in the *Believer*
"High-Functioning" in *Buzzfeed Reader*
"The Choice of Children" in *Doll Hospital*
"Reality, On-Screen" in the *New Inquiry*
"Perdition Days" in the *Toast*
"L'Appel du Vide" in *Hazlitt*

This publication is made possible, in part, by the voters of Minnesota through a Minnesota State Arts Board Operating Support grant, thanks to a legislative appropriation from the arts and cultural heritage fund, and a grant from the Wells Fargo Foundation. Significant support has also been provided by the National Endowment for the Arts, Target, the McKnight Foundation, the Lannan Foundation, the Amazon Literary Partnership, and other generous contributions from foundations, corporations, and individuals. To these organizations and individuals we offer our heartfelt thanks.

Published by Graywolf Press
250 Third Avenue North, Suite 600
Minneapolis, Minnesota 55401

www.graywolfpress.org

Published in the United States of America

ISBN 978-1-55597-827-3

10 12 14 15 13 11

Library of Congress Control Number: 2018947092

Cover design: Kimberly Glyder

Cover art: Shutterstock

for Chris

&

for everyone who has been touched by the schizophrenias

Recovery [from schizophrenia], almost never complete, runs the gamut from a level tolerable to society to one that may not require permanent hospitalization but in fact does not allow even the semblance of normal life. More than any symptom, the defining characteristic of the illness is the profound feeling of incomprehensibility and inaccessibility that sufferers provoke in other people.
—Sylvia Nasar, *A Beautiful Mind*

How can I go on this way?
And how can I not?
—Susan Sontag

Contents

THE
COLLECTED
SCHIZOPHRENIAS

Diagnosis

Schizophrenia terrifies. It is the archetypal disorder of lunacy. Craziness scares us because we are creatures who long for structure and sense; we divide the interminable days into years, months, and weeks. We hope for ways to corral and control bad fortune, illness, unhappiness, discomfort, and death—all inevitable outcomes that we pretend are anything but. And still, the fight against entropy seems wildly futile in the face of schizophrenia, which shirks reality in favor of its own internal logic.

People speak of schizophrenics as though they were dead without being dead, gone in the eyes of those around them. Schizophrenics are victims of the Russian word гибель (*gibel*), which is synonymous with "doom" and "catastrophe"—not necessarily death nor suicide, but a ruinous cessation of existence; we deteriorate in a way that is painful for others. Psychoanalyst Christopher Bollas defines "schizophrenic presence" as the psychodynamic experience of "being with [a schizophrenic] who has seemingly crossed over from the human world to the non-human environment," because other human catastrophes can bear the weight of human narrative—war, kidnapping, death—but schizophrenia's built-in chaos resists sense. Both *gibel* and "schizophrenic presence" address the suffering of those who are adjacent to the one who is suffering in the first place.

Because the schizophrenic does suffer. I have been psychically lost in a pitch-dark room. There is the ground, which may be nowhere other than immediately below my own numbed feet. Those foot-shaped anchors are the only trustworthy landmarks. If I make a wrong move, I'll have to face the gruesome consequence. In this bleak abyss the key is to not be afraid, because fear, though inevitable, only compounds the awful feeling of being lost.

According to the National Institute of Mental Health (NIMH), schizophrenia afflicts 1.1 percent of the American adult population. The number grows when considering the full psychotic spectrum, also known as "the schizophrenias": 0.3 percent[1] of the American population are diagnosed with schizoaffective disorder; 3.9 percent[2] are diagnosed with schizotypal personality disorder. I am aware of the implications of the word "afflicts," which supports a neurotypical bias, but I also believe in the suffering of people diagnosed with the schizophrenias and our tormenting minds.

I was officially diagnosed with schizoaffective disorder, bipolar type eight years after experiencing my first hallucinations, back when I first suspected fresh hell in my brain. I remain surprised by how long it took. I was diagnosed with bipolar disorder in 2001, but heard my first auditory hallucination—a voice—in 2005, in my early twenties. I knew enough about abnormal psychology to understand that people with bipolar disorder could experience symptoms of

---

1. The National Alliance on Mental Illness.
2. Daniel R. Rosell et al., "Schizotypal Personality Disorder: A Current Review," *Current Psychiatry Reports* 16.7 (2014): 452. PMC. Web. 26 Oct. 2017.

psychosis, but were not supposed to experience them outside of a mood episode. I communicated this to Dr. C, my psychiatrist at the time, but she never uttered the words "schizoaffective disorder," even when I reported that I was dodging invisible demons on campus, and that I'd watched a fully formed locomotive roar toward me before vanishing. I began to call these experiences "sensory distortions," a phrase that Dr. C readily adopted in my presence instead of "hallucinations," which was what they were.

Some people dislike diagnoses, disagreeably calling them boxes and labels, but I've always found comfort in preexisting conditions; I like to know that I'm not pioneering an inexplicable experience. For years, I hinted to Dr. C that schizoaffective disorder might be a more accurate diagnosis for me than bipolar disorder, but to no avail. I believe she was wary of officially shifting me from the more common terrain of mood and anxiety disorders to the wilds of the schizophrenias, which would subject me to self-censure and stigma from others—including those with access to my diagnostic chart. Dr. C continued to treat my condition with mood stabilizers and antipsychotics for the next eight years, never once suggesting that my illness might be something else. Then I began to truly fall apart, and switched to a new psychiatrist. Dr. M reluctantly diagnosed me as having schizoaffective disorder, bipolar type, which remains my primary psychiatric diagnosis. It is a label that I am okay with, for now.

A diagnosis is comforting because it provides a framework—a community, a lineage—and, if luck is afoot, a treatment or cure. A diagnosis says that I am crazy, but in a particular way: one that has been experienced and recorded not just in modern times, but also by the ancient Egyptians, who described a condition similar to schizophrenia in the Book of Hearts, and attributed psychosis to the dangerous influence of poison in the heart and uterus. The ancient

Egyptians understood the importance of sighting patterns of behavior. Uterus, hysteria; heart, a looseness of association. They saw the utility of giving those patterns names.

My diagnosis of schizoaffective disorder, bipolar type resulted from a series of messages between my psychiatrist and myself, sent through my HMO's website.

From: Wang, Esmé Weijun
Sent: 2/19/2013 9:28 a.m. PST
To: Dr. M

unfortunately i have not been doing well for a few days (since sunday)
by end of sunday i was upset because the day had passed in a "fog," i.e. i could not account for what i had done all day despite having painstakingly [made] a list of what i had done that day, i could not remember having done anything, it was like i had "lost time"; i was also very tired and took 2 naps (i did not take any more klonopin than usual that day, in fact i would say i took less, maybe 2 mgs)
monday i realized i was having the same problem; trouble functioning at work, especially with concentration, i would stare at the same sentence for a long time and it would not make sense; i took a nap on a couch in the office; again i felt the day had passed without my existing in it; by 4 i was unsure that i was real or that anything else was real, also having concerns with whether i had a face, but not wanting to look to see if i had a face and feeling agitated at the prospect of other faces. symptoms cont. today

From: Dr. M

Received: 2/19/2013 12:59 p.m. PST

Ok, just re-read this again—definitely sounds more like psychosis is the problem. Increasing seroquel could be the answer (to 1.5 pills—max dose is 800 mgs). I think you may have schizoaffective disorder—a slightly different variant than bipolar I.

Btw, have you read Elyn Saks's The Center Cannot Hold? I'd be curious to know your thoughts about it

Years later, I read between the lines of Dr. M's brief response. She describes schizoaffective disorder as "a slightly different variant than bipolar I," but does not specify what she means by "variant"—a variant of what? Schizophrenia and bipolar disorder are both considered *Diagnostic and Statistical Manual* Axis I, or *DSM* clinical disorders; perhaps "variant" refers to that broad realm, which includes the worlds of depression and anxiety in its geography.

Dr. M tosses in, as though it's an afterthought, a mention of the most well-known schizophrenia memoir of the last thirty years, written by MacArthur Genius Grant winner Elyn R. Saks. The mention of Saks is a potential buffer for her bad news of a terrible diagnosis. It can also be seen as Dr. M's way of emphasizing normalcy: you may have schizoaffective disorder, *but we can still talk about books.* In fact, in four years schizoaffective disorder will be a diagnosis that Ron Powers, in his hefty examination of schizophrenia titled *No One Cares about Crazy People*, will repeatedly call worse than schizophrenia, and in four years, I will draw exclamation points in the margins and argue with Powers in pencil. And yet there is also a predecessor for me to admire: Saks, who used her MacArthur money to create a think tank for issues affecting mental health, for whom schizophrenia has shaped her calling. Those who like to chirrup that "everything happens for a reason" might point to Saks's research and advocacy, which likely would never have happened had she been born neurotypical, as part of God's plan.

This is how the *Diagnostic and Statistical Manual* (*DSM-5*), a clinical bible created by the American Psychiatric Association (APA), describes schizophrenia:

Schizophrenia, 295.90 (F20.9)

A. Two (or more) of the following, each present for a significant portion of time during a 1-month period (or less if successfully treated). At least one of these[3] must be (1), (2), or (3):

1. Delusions.

2. Hallucinations.

3. Disorganized speech (e.g., frequent derailment or incoherence).

4. Grossly disorganized or catatonic[4] behavior.

5. Negative symptoms (i.e., diminished emotional expression or avolition).

B. For a significant portion of the time since the onset of the disturbance, level of functioning[5] in one or more major areas, such as work, interpersonal relations, or self-care, is markedly below the level achieved prior to the onset (or

---

3. The first two are symptoms of psychosis. I have yet to experience the third.

4. Catatonic behavior in the clinical sense is not the same as catatonia in the layman's sense. According to the *DSM-5*, catatonia can also include excessive motor activity.

5. To be diagnosed with schizophrenia, a person must be low-functioning, though a person living well with schizophrenia may also be considered high-functioning.

when the onset is in childhood or adolescence, there is failure to achieve expected level of interpersonal, academic, or occupational functioning).

C. Continuous signs of the disturbance persist for at least 6 months. This 6-month period must include at least 1 month of symptoms (or less if successfully treated) that meet Criterion A (i.e., active-phase symptoms) and may include periods of prodomal or residual symptoms. During these prodomal or residual periods, the signs of the disturbance may be manifested by only negative symptoms or by two or more symptoms listed in Criterion A present in an attenuated form (e.g., odd beliefs, unusual perceptual experiences).

D. Schizoaffective disorder and depressive or bipolar disorder with psychotic features have been ruled out because either 1) no major depressive or manic episodes have occurred concurrently with the active-phase symptoms, or 2) if mood episodes have occurred during active-phase symptoms, they have been present for a minority of the total duration of the active and residual periods of the illness.

E. The disturbance is not attributable to the physiological effects of a substance (e.g., a drug of abuse, a medication) or another medical condition.

F. If there is a history of autism spectrum disorder or a communication disorder of childhood onset, the additional diagnosis of schizophrenia is made only if prominent delusions or hallucinations, in addition to the other required symptoms of schizophrenia, are also present for at least 1 month (or less if successfully treated).

Clinicians use these guidelines in order to discern the presence of schizophrenia. Medicine is an inexact science, but psychiatry is particularly so. There is no blood test, no genetic marker to determine beyond a shadow of a doubt that someone is schizophrenic, and schizophrenia itself is nothing more or less than a constellation of symptoms that have frequently been observed as occurring in tandem. Observing patterns and giving them names is helpful mostly if those patterns can speak to a common cause or, better yet, a common treatment or cure.

Schizophrenia is the most familiar of the psychotic disorders. Schizoaffective disorder is less familiar to the layperson, and so I have a ready song-and-dance that I use to explain it. I've quipped onstage to thousands that schizoaffective disorder is the fucked-up offspring of manic depression and schizophrenia, though this is not quite accurate; because schizoaffective disorder must include a major mood episode, the disorder may combine mania and schizophrenia, or depression and schizophrenia. Its diagnostic criteria, according to the *DSM-5*, read as follows:

Schizoaffective Disorder, Bipolar type 295.70 (F25.0) This subtype applies if a manic episode is part of the presentation. Major depressive episodes may also occur.

A. An uninterrupted period of illness during which there is a major mood episode (major depression or manic) concurrent with Criterion A of schizophrenia. Note: The major depressive episode must include Criterion A1: Depressed mood.

B. Delusions or hallucinations for 2 or more weeks in the absence of a major mood episode (depressive or manic) during the lifetime duration of the illness.

C. Symptoms that meet criteria for a major mood episode are present for the majority of the total duration of the active and residual portions of the illness.

D. The disturbance is not attributable to the effects of a substance (e.g., a drug of abuse, a medication) or another medical condition.

To read the *DSM-5* definition of my felt experience is to be cast far from the horror of psychosis and an unbridled mood; it shrinkwraps the bloody circumstance with objectivity until the words are colorless. I received the new diagnosis of schizoaffective disorder after twelve years of being considered bipolar, in the middle of a psychiatric crisis that went on for ten months. By then, the trees had long shed their dead leaves. But in the beginning of 2013, the psychosis was young. I had months to go of a frequent erasure of time; a loss of feeling toward family, as though they had been replaced by doubles (known as Capgras delusion); the inability to read a page of words, and so forth, which meant that the agitation I felt at realizing something was badly wrong would only go on and on and on and on.

Though the German physician Emil Kraepelin is credited with pinpointing the disorder he called "dementia praecox" in 1893, it was Swiss psychiatrist Eugen Bleuler who coined the word "schizophrenia" in 1908. Bleuler derived the term from the Greek roots *schizo* ("split") and *phrene* ("mind") to address the "loosening of associations" that are common in the disorder. The notion of a split mind has led to a lousy—as in, both ableist and inaccurate—integration of "schizophrenia" into the vernacular. In a 2013 *Slate* article titled "*Schizophrenic* Is the New *Retarded*," neuroscientist Patrick House noted that "a stock market can be schizophrenic when volatile, a politician when breaking from party lines, a composer when dissonant, a tax code when contradictory, weather when inclement, or a rapper when headlining as a poet." In other words, schizophrenia is confusing, off-putting, nonsensical, unpredictable, inexplicable, and just plain bad. Schizophrenia is also conflated with dissociative identity disorder, more commonly known as multiple personality disorder, due to the vernacular use of "split personality" to refer to a disorder unrelated to fractured personalities. And though psychosis is a phenomenon shared by disorders other than schizophrenia, the words "psycho" and "psychotic" are used to refer to everything from obnoxious ex-girlfriends to bloodthirsty serial killers.

Though Bleuler's coinage is his most enduring legacy, he also went on to conduct the bulk of pioneering work on schizophrenia, including the seminal monograph *Dementia Praecox, or The Group of Schizophrenias*. As Victor Peralta and Manuel J. Cuesta describe in "Eugen Bleuler and the Schizophrenias: 100 Years After" (*Schizophrenia Bulletin*), Bleuler conceived of schizophrenias as a "genus rather than a species." As a concept, the schizophrenias encompass a range of psychotic disorders, and it is a genus that I choose to identify with as a woman whose diagnosis is unfamiliar to most— the shaggy, sharp-toothed thing, and not the wolf.

The *DSM* is published by the APA, which released its long-awaited, updated "bible for mental disorders," the *DSM-5*, in May 2013. Updates to the *DSM* aren't set like clockwork; after all, the *DSM-IV* wasn't released until 1994, and the *DSM-III*, which infamously contained the diagnosis of "ego-dystonic homosexuality," came out in 1980. I'm not a psychiatrist, psychologist, or therapist, but I am a patient whose life is affected by the labels that the *DSM* provides, and so I was curious to see what, other than the switch from roman to arabic numerals, would change. After all, it is easy to forget that psychiatric diagnoses are human constructs, and not handed down from an all-knowing God on stone tablets; to "have schizophrenia" is to fit an assemblage of symptoms, which are listed in a purple book made by humans.

With the arrival of the *DSM-5* came the psychiatric bible's most significant change: not the actual diagnoses within the *DSM*, nor the symptoms that make up the diagnoses, but rather the idea of defining psychiatry itself. NIMH, a component of the US Department of Health and Human Services—immortalized by the 1982 animated movie *The Secret of NIMH*, which depicts the organization as a sinister and unethical entity—shifted the landscape by decreeing that the *DSM* is "no longer sufficient for researchers," according to NIMH director Thomas Insel. No longer would the APA and NIMH stand together in a uniform discussion of "what psychiatry is"; rather, NIMH declared that it was, and had been, striking out on its own.

Psychiatry emphasizes a clinician's judgment as the primary tool for diagnosis. Someone suffering from mental health complaints may first be given a blood test or a brain scan by a primary care physician. If those tests come back clean, it's the psychiatrist's role to ask questions intended to suss out whether the sick person qualifies for one of the hundreds of diagnoses delineated by the *DSM*, all of which rely on groups of symptoms and sighted or self-reported patterns. (The disorders are indexed with decimal numbers, making the endeavor seem even more capital-*S* Scientific. I spent much of my adolescence squinting at the numbers on my charts, trying to memorize them so that I could look them up later. Schizophrenia is 295.90; my diagnosis of schizoaffective disorder, bipolar type is 295.70 [F25.0].) Humans are the arbiters of which diagnoses are given to other humans—who are, in most cases, suffering, and at the mercy of doctors whose diagnostic decisions hold great power. Giving someone a diagnosis of schizophrenia will impact how they see themselves. It will change how they interact with friends and family. The diagnosis will affect how they are seen by the medical community, the legal system, the Transportation Security Administration, and so on.

The most common complaint about the *DSM-5*, and the *DSM* versions that came before it, is that the disorders it lists are based on clusters of symptoms rather than objective measures. I realized just how arbitrary such definitions are in practice while working as a lab manager at the Stanford Department of Psychology, where I ran clinical interviews to assess potential subjects for study. At the time, Stanford's Mood and Anxiety Disorders Laboratory relied on the Structured Clinical Interview for *DSM-IV*, or SCID, to determine whether someone qualified for the diagnosis we were trying to research. I went through a year of training, including months of practicing phone interviews, taking a written test, running through a battery of simulated interviews with coworkers, and supervision during several official interviews, until I was qualified to run the two- to three-hour-long SCIDs alone.

To "run a SCID" means taking a potential subject through a battery of questions taken from the SCID binder—a hefty stack of paper with a spine several inches wide. The interview begins by collecting preliminary demographic information, and goes on to run a person through a diagnostic flowchart. For example, "Did you ever hear things that other people couldn't hear, such as noises, or the voices of people whispering or talking? Were you awake at the time?" moves on to "What did you hear? How often did you hear it?" if the answer is yes. If the answer is no, the next question becomes "Did you ever have visions or see things that other people couldn't see? Were you awake at the time? How long were they present?" At the end of the interview, the researcher determines the interviewee's primary diagnosis, and writes it on the front in ink.

In our lab, running SCIDs was not only the most prestigious task an employee could do but also the most emotionally draining.

Running a single SCID often meant listening to a litany of someone's most excruciating experiences and memories. We were not
permitted to cry during these interviews, but I often bit back tears
during the most intense of them. It was frustrating to see interviewees
come in and reveal an underbelly of bloody wounds, only to have to
turn them away from participating in the experiments for which
they'd applied, and often for what seemed like insignificant reasons.
An Eeyore-esque man who wept at random and clearly seemed depressed could be eliminated from our "major depressive disorder"
(MDD) subject pool for not meeting the full criteria. According to
the *DSM-IV*, he would need to meet five or more of a list of nine
symptoms—including fatigue or loss of energy, weight loss or gain,
or feelings of worthlessness—for most of the time during the same
two-week period. At least one of the symptoms would have to be
a depressed mood, or a loss of interest or pleasure (known as anhedonia). If the depressed person had only four of the nine symptoms, or came into our office at the one-and-a-half-week mark, he
would be recorded as "sub-MDD," because it was not a therapeutic
clinic but a research lab, where our subjects needed to be as "clean"
as possible—and doing hundreds, if not thousands, of interviews
made it clear to me that diagnoses were rarely cut-and-dried.

As a researcher, I lacked the luxury of being able to bend criteria. However, psychiatrists can, given that their job is to ameliorate
symptoms and the suffering that accompanies them, rather than to
find, diagnose, and study spotless instances of any given disorder.
A psychiatrist attempting to make a diagnosis might go through a
flowchart similar to the one that the SCID comprises. They might
ask, using plainspoken language, the same questions found in the
weighty binders I carried from the interview room to the main
office; but someone that I would have labeled "sub-MDD" would
likely be diagnosed by a psychiatrist as clinically depressed, with a

Prozac prescription not far behind. Clinical flexibility has its benefits. It also has the potential for human error, as well as the ability to harm.

With the advent of new technologies and genetic research, psychiatry is increasingly turning toward biology, with NIMH leading the charge. In a press release about the *DSM-5*, published on April 29, 2013, NIMH spoke about the so-called weakness of the *DSM*'s categorizations made via observed or reported clusters of symptoms, announcing that "patients with mental disorders deserve better." Simultaneously, NIMH promoted its own project—a surprise to those outside of the scientific community—called the Research Domain Criteria project, or RDoC. RDoC's aim, according to the 2008 NIMH Strategic Plan, is to "develop, for research purposes, new ways of classifying mental disorders based on dimensions of observable behavior and neurobiological measures." In other words: let's bring more hard science to psychiatry.

Identical twins, according to seminal twin studies in the 1960s, have only a 40 to 50 percent chance of both developing schizophrenia, despite their shared genes. According to the diathesis-stress model of psychiatric illness, a genetic vulnerability to a disorder blooms only if enough stressors cause those vulnerable genes to express themselves. When I worked as a lab manager, we researchers spoke of the possibility that our studies might one day bear practical fruit. Someday we might be able to inform parents of their children's genetic risk for mental illness, and those parents might be able to employ preventive measures before the first signs made themselves apparent. We did not discuss the practicalities or ethics of taking such action.

Some stressors appear to be prenatal. People diagnosed with schizophrenia are more likely to be born in the winter than in the summer, perhaps due to maternal infection during pregnancy—I was born in the swelter of a Midwestern June. Difficult births, obstetrical complications, and stressful events suffered by the mother, such as assault and war, are also correlated. My head had lodged behind a bone in my mother's pelvis, which hints of an intergenerational transmission of trauma; stress causes the flooding of cortisol and other chemicals into the brain, and my newly immigrated, newly married young mother had her own psychiatric issues to contend with. Who knows what happens to the malleable and muddy assortment of fetal cells because of such strain?

Once during a train ride in Taiwan with my mother, I asked her about my great-aunt, who I knew had been insane. On the small, pull-down lap desk, my mother placed a notebook and sketched a family tree. She drew X's to signify those known to have some sort of mental illness. What surprised me weren't so much the three X's that did exist—the great-aunt who'd been institutionalized for most of her life, despite having been a first-generation college student, and who lived a tragic existence as the madwoman in the attic; my mother's cousin who had killed himself, ostensibly after a bad breakup; and, of course, me—but rather how many unknown entities there were, with branches leading to blank spaces on the page. "No one talks about these things," she said. "No one wants to question what genetic legacies might lurk in our bloodline." When asked point-blank by my first psychiatrist, over a decade ago, whether there was mental illness in the family, my mother said no, there was nothing. Even now, she doesn't consider herself an X on the family tree, preferring to keep herself a mild circle, absolved on the page despite her own history of suicidal ideation, panic, and hiding in closets. My father's side of the family has other concerns, primarily addiction, but is not considered responsible for my so-called bad genes. I've inherited a love of writing and a talent for the visual arts from my mother, as well as her long and tapered fingers; I've also inherited a tendency for madness.

The APA's response to this ill-timed potshot from NIMH came in the form of a statement from the chair of the *DSM-5* Task Force, David Kupfer. Kupfer publicly responded that RDoC "may someday . . . revolutionize our field," but added that people with mental illness are suffering in the present moment. Having biological and genetic markers as diagnostic tools would be wonderful, but "this promise, which we had anticipated since the 1970s, remains disappointingly distant. . . . [The *DSM-5*] represents the strongest system currently available for classifying disorders." Speaking directly to the urgency of public need, Kupfer said, "Our patients deserve no less."

What is perhaps most interesting about the RDoC announcement, however, is just how complex an RDoC-*DSM* marriage might become—and it's a problem that researchers are working on solving. Dr. Sheri Johnson, professor of psychology at the University of California, Berkeley, said to me, "I think we are a long way away from that marriage. RDoC is a fascinating initiative, but it's really designed to help us understand some of the key neurobiological dimensions involved in mental health. There's a lot of work to be done . . . Once we have those dimensions more clearly mapped, it may shift the way we think about diagnosis enough that we won't really be using the same types of categories that appear in [the] *DSM*."

Dr. Victor Reus, a professor of psychiatry at the University of California, San Francisco, and psychiatrist, is similarly skeptical about the use of biomarkers as diagnostic or clinical tools—at least until genetic research grows by leaps and bounds. "I think trying to do biomarkers of schizophrenia as an entity is probably a hopeless task," Reus told me in an interview, "because there are just so many different ways in which people can develop a syndrome that looks like schizophrenia, or that fulfills the criteria of schizophrenia as we now define it." And yet this may not be the case for other disorders. "Certain categories," Reus states, "as crude as they are, are still useful in capturing a group of individuals that probably have more in common in terms of etiology or basic mechanism than they are different. And certain disorders are better than others in that regard. So autism has proven to be a pretty useful thing. Bipolar disorder has proven to be, I think, more useful than schizophrenia. Obsessive-compulsive disorder is probably one of the more specific ones. Major depression is problematic. Generalized anxiety disorder is very problematic."

As of 2017, NIMH continues to vigorously fund research into the schizophrenias. The 2017 NIMH budget describes an increase of $6 million (up to a total of $15.5 million) for programs designed to address psychosis and its treatment; the goal of initiatives such as Recovery After an Initial Schizophrenia Episode (RAISE) and the Early Psychosis Intervention Network (EPINET) is to "ensure that lessons learned from research and clinical experiences are systematically and rapidly put to use to improve [lives]."

For now, psychiatrists continue to rely on the *DSM*, and on the *DSM-5*, which means that changes in the bible of psychiatry continue to affect people's lives. The definition of "schizophrenia" changed with the *DSM-5*. Schizophrenia's subtypes—paranoid, disorganized, catatonic, and undifferentiated—no longer exist in the new *DSM*, which means, among other things, that pop culture has lost "paranoid schizophrenia" as a diagnosis upon which to hang criminal acts. The five key symptoms are listed as: (1) delusions, (2) hallucinations, (3) disorganized speech, (4) disorganized or catatonic behavior, and (5) "negative" symptoms (symptoms that detract, such as avolition). A person must now demonstrate at least two of the specified symptoms; previously, only one symptom was required. At least one "positive" symptom—delusions, hallucinations, disorganized speech—must be present.

Schizoaffective disorder changed as well. When I first heard that its criteria had been altered, my nerves twitched—had my diagnosis been erased? If the diagnosis hadn't been erased, would my association with it be, if I no longer fit the criteria? But as I skimmed "Highlights of Changes from *DSM-IV-TR* to *DSM-5*," a PDF created by the APA to accompany the *DSM-5*'s release, I realized that I still fit the mold. According to the document, "The primary change to schizoaffective disorder is the requirement that a major mood episode be present *for a majority of the disorder's total duration after Criteria A has been met*" (italics mine).

In "Schizoaffective Disorder in the *DSM-5*," Dolores Malaspina et al. explain these changes by pointing out that psychotic symptoms and mood episodes frequently happen at the same time. A person with bipolar disorder may experience psychosis during a manic or depressive episode; a person with major depression may experience psychosis during their depression. As a result, schizoaffective disorder was diagnosed more often than warranted for a diagnostic category that "was originally intended to [only] rarely [be] needed."

The new *DSM* definition of schizoaffective disorder is intended to look at a lifetime of illness, and not an episode of illness; a longitudinal look at schizoaffective disorder means that there must be at least one two-week period of psychosis *without* clinical mood symptoms, and full mood disorder episodes must have been present "from the onset of psychotic symptoms up until the current diagnosis." In other words, schizoaffective disorder is intended to be an uncommon diagnosis, and it is meant to be diagnosed based on a lifetime of illness—both of which will be true if the *DSM-5* does its job. Under its auspices, I remain a rare bird who, according to the APA, will likely be sick forever. The *DSM* is what we use to define the problem, yes, but it attempts to do so in a way that accommodates humanity's wide and nuanced spectrum, which may not be a realistic goal. If I were still a researcher studying *DSM-IV* or *DSM-5* categories, grant proposals to NIMH would need to include something about the implications for RDoC. However, NIMH's public rejection of the *DSM-5* has no impact on me as a layperson, or on my insurance company, my therapist, or my psychiatrist. And although blood tests or brain scans for mental illness diagnoses are either far-off or never to come, RDoC's first benefits may give us a better sense of what biological features mark susceptibility to already established disorders, as well as what types of stressors are most likely to transform those susceptibilities into illness.

I remain skeptical that we'll see either outcome in my lifetime. I am accustomed to the world of the *DSM*, which remains the heavy purple bible-o'-madness that sits on a clinician's shelf. It is, like the Judeo-Christian bible, one that warps and mutates as quickly as our culture does. The *DSM* defines problems so that we can determine whether a person fits into them, or whether a person has lapsed out of the problem entirely—which is not to say that their life changes, even if their label does.

For causes and explanations, there are still other avenues to pursue. Nine months after my diagnosis of schizoaffective disorder, when I was beginning to experience serious physical symptoms as well— fainting, chronic pain, allergies, weakness—my psychiatrist sent me to a complementary and alternative medicine (CAM) consult, a division within my HMO. The doctor, a Southeast Asian man, looked at my tongue. He used the Chinese three-finger method of examining the pulse in both of my wrists. He told me that my problem was obvious: it was a classic case of a Fire typology that had burned out of control, therefore explaining my ambitious personality, pain, inflammation, anxiety, depression, and symptoms of schizophrenia. He indicated a few acupressure points that I could try, including one in the dip of my sternum called the Sea of Tranquility. He advised me to eat less meat and fewer spices. I sipped a chai latte from a to-go cup in his office, and between sips I became anxious that he would smell the chai on my breath, and chide me for feeding an already raging conflagration.

Later I consulted *Beyond Heaven and Earth: A Guide to Chinese Medicine*, by Harriet Beinfield, LAc, and Efrem Korngold, LAc, OMD, which explains that when the Qi of the Fire type is too strong, "the *Qi* of the *Heart* can attack the *Lung*, . . . leaving the envelope of the skin open and loose, unable to guard the body and contain the *Essence* and *Spirit*." Resulting emotional problems include the person's "[becoming] restless and sensitive—easily moved from laughter to tears and prone toward melancholy and anxiety." A condition recognizable as psychosis may also result, as the authors warn about "altered states of perception in which reality becomes plastic and fluctuating." To identify as a Fire type, in the same way that I might identify as a Myers-Briggs INFJ or a Gemini with Capricorn rising, is to accept the baseline Fire characteristics of being intuitive and empathetic, and believing in the power of charisma, as well as risking the Fire problems of "anxiety, agitation, and frenzy" and "bizarre perceptions and sensations."

This period of acute and terrible illness in the winter of 2013, ultimately diagnosed in 2015 as late-stage Lyme disease, resulted in genetic testing for an MTHFR mutation, and came with a wealth of extra information. Based on preliminary research of a marker at rs833497 in the DYM gene, my CC genotype places me at "slightly higher odds" of schizophrenia, as opposed to CT (also "slightly higher odds") or TT ("typical odds").

Sometimes I encounter people who don't believe in mental illness. These people may have been diagnosed with depression or anxiety at some point, but are usually symptom-free when I meet them. Often, they claim that such diagnoses are oppressive to those with unique abilities. To these people, "unique abilities" usually suggests those conferred by psychosis. They will cite John Nash, who has said that the same mind that produced his delusions produced his brilliant ideas. I am frequently told with great sincerity that in other cultures, a person who would be diagnosed with schizophrenia in the West might be lauded as a shaman and healer. *Have you ever considered,* they ask, *that schizophrenia might be a spiritual characteristic, and not a malady?* Often these people declare that they don't believe in medicine. They are likely to be the type who boast about never taking aspirin for a headache. I mention these people with some cynicism, but I, too, have wondered if my experiences with psychosis are a spiritual gift rather than a psychiatric anomaly.

In 2014 an astrologer visited me at my cottage in the woods, where I was staying during a writing residency. Since Neptune was conjoined to my ascendant, Saturn was conjoined to Pluto, and Taurus was in my fourth House, she informed me that I was susceptible to intense dreams and psychic abilities. Due to my fragile energetic field, she said, I would be well advised to live a gentle life. Another astrologer, whom I consulted for a second opinion, informed me that the Neptune conjunction is a dramatic placement. "Neptune is divinity; it is access to the gods," she said. "But no one ever came out of a conversation with the gods for the better, right?"

In 2016 I enrolled in a yearlong program in the so-called sacred arts, also known as syncretic mysticism, or, less accurately, witchcraft. The instructor for the course in magic—a woman with a sweet voice and a lineage of sacred artistry—suggested that I study the liminal, which is the theme running through the psycho-spiritual claim that I am sensitive to the thin skin between the otherworld and that which we call reality, the "fragile energetic field," the "access to the gods."

These are what I call explanations, rather than causes, because embedded within spiritual narratives are ideas about Why with a capital *W*, providing larger, more-cosmic reasons for the schizo-phrenias to occur.

We could consider the role of evolution as yet another kind of cosmic reasoning. Researchers such as Steve Dorus, an evolution-ary geneticist at Syracuse University and the coauthor of the paper "Adaptive Evolution in Genes Defining Schizophrenia," devote their careers to investigating schizophrenia's curious evolutionary persistence. Despite schizophrenics' reduced reproductive fitness (defined as an individual's reproductive success, as well as their av-erage contribution to the gene pool), Dorus et al. have noticed that twenty-eight of seventy-six gene variations connected to schizo-phrenia are actually preferred. One potential explanation suggests that the evolutionary development of speech, language, and crea-tivity, while bestowing significant gifts, has "dragged" along less desirable genetic tendencies with it; from this perspective, schizo-phrenia is simply the price humanity pays for the ability to write heartrending operas and earthshaking speeches. Another argu-ment: schizophrenics are, evolutionarily, meant to be ad hoc "cult leaders" whose bizarre ideas split off chunks of the human popula-tion. This in itself is neither bad nor good, though one's perspective on the matter could depend on whether one believes cults or cultish ideas are inherently bad or good.

Or we could say that schizophrenia *itself* has evolutionary advantages. Some have suggested that schizophrenia persists because it promotes creativity, much like the argument emphasized in MacArthur Genius Grant winner Kay Redfield Jamison's *Touched with Fire: Manic-Depressive Illness and the Artistic Temperament*. As tempting as this perspective is, I worry that seeing schizophrenia as a gateway to artistic brilliance glamorizes the disorder in unhealthy ways, therefore preventing suffering schizophrenics from seeking help. If creativity is more important than being able to maintain a sense of reality, I could make a plausible argument for remaining psychotic, but the price of doing so is one that neither I nor my loved ones are likely to choose to pay.

In these investigations of why and how, I am hoping to uncover an origin story. Pan Gu the giant slept in an egg-shaped cloud; once released, he formed the world with his blood, bones, and flesh. God said, "Let there be light." Ymir was fed by a cow who came from ice. Because *How did this come to be?* is another way of asking, *Why did this happen?*, which is another way of asking, *What do I do now? But what on earth do I do now?*

Toward a Pathology
of the Possessed

Of the details reported about the murder of Malcoum Tate, a thirty-four-year-old man who was killed by his younger sister at the side of the road late at night while their mother waited in the car, most striking is the fact that his sister shot him thirteen times. On December 18, 1988, Lothell Tate, thirty-two, used a .25 caliber weapon that required her to shoot, reload the seven-round magazine, and shoot again to hit her brother a full thirteen times in the head and back. Lothell and her mother, Pauline Wilkerson, checked for a pulse, and then they rolled Malcoum's body into a gully before driving home to Gastonia, North Carolina.

As word of the crime spread, headlines from newspapers such as the *Lakeland Ledger*, the *Herald-Journal*, and the *Charlotte Observer* provided a framework for Lothell Tate and Pauline Wilkerson's motivations. Headlines read, "NC Family's Final Solution Was Murder," "Family's Nightmare Ends with Slaying of Problem Child," and "Death Ends Family's Nightmare." The "nightmare" was a life starring their blood relation as a persistent threat—a man diagnosed with severe paranoid schizophrenia who had been hospitalized again and again and again and who had been jailed for assault, but who resisted medication and, according to anecdote, repeatedly threatened his family like a ghoulish specter. It is reported that Malcoum claimed Lothell's two-year-old daughter had the devil in her, and that God had sent him to kill her; apparently, Malcoum loomed over their beds at night till either Lothell or Pauline startled awake, upon which he would laugh a "crazy laugh" and leave the room.

National Book Award–winning author Andrew Solomon describes schizophrenia in his 2012 book, *Far from the Tree: Parents, Children, and the Search for Identity*, as "like Alzheimer's . . . an illness not of accrual but of replacement and deletion; rather than obscuring the previously known person, this disease to some degree eliminates that person." Though there is no direct reference for this statement in the book's extensive notes, his description remains a lyrical summary of how schizophrenia is commonly understood. Brain-imaging studies of patients with schizophrenia have shown a reduced volume of gray matter, as well as ventricular enlargement. In a BBC interview with Professor Paul Thompson of UCLA, such examples of tissue damage are described as "[moving] across the brain like a forest fire, destroying more tissue as the disease [progresses]."

Schizophrenia's unpleasant prognosis today, as described by researchers like Thompson, is essentially the same as it was in the time of Emil Kraepelin and, later, as described by Eugen Bleuler. "Dementia praecox" was a progressive and neurodegenerative disease, unlike manic depression, or what we now call bipolar disorder. Kraepelin is credited for revealing that manic depression, which may also exhibit psychotic symptoms, is a fundamentally different disorder from what's now called schizophrenia, and is also a disorder that does not, unlike schizophrenia, lead to a permanently damaged brain.

In 2013 I experienced a seven-month-long psychotic episode as a symptom of schizoaffective disorder, which I'd been diagnosed with that February. Beginning in 2002, I had tried every atypical antipsychotic on the market—atypical antipsychotics being the pharmaceutical family of choice for psychosis, proving less likely to cause the severe side effects of their predecessors—and yet none of those medications had worked for me. Even Clorazil, considered to be the powerful antipsychotic of last resort due to its ability to cause a lethal plummet in white blood cell count in some people, hadn't been effective in eliminating my delusions. I was terrified and concerned; my family was worried and concerned; my doctor was perplexed and concerned. Dr. M told me that the longer the episode lasted, and the more frequently the episodes occurred, the more damage was occurring to my brain.

It is disconcerting for anyone to be told that her brain is being damaged by an uncontrollable illness. It might have been especially disconcerting to me because my brain has been one of my more valuable assets since childhood. I began to read at two; I was the first student, boy or girl, to finish every available math textbook in my elementary school; I went to Yale and Stanford, and graduated from Stanford with a 3.99 GPA, after which I took a job as a lab manager and researcher at one of the university's brain-imaging labs. My anxiety about a loss of gray matter fed a variety of delusions: one afternoon I frantically called my husband at work to babble about spiders eating holes in my brain. And so I took Solomon's words like a punch in the gut, but his statement about "replacement and deletion" reflects a common narrative about schizophrenia, a narrative unlike those about psychiatric diagnoses such as depression or obsessive-compulsive disorder. The story of schizophrenia is one with a protagonist, "the schizophrenic," who is first a fine and good vessel with fine and good things inside of it, and then becomes misshapen through the ravages of psychosis; the vessel becomes prone to being filled with nasty things. Finally, the wicked thoughts and behavior that may ensue become inseparable from the person, who is now unrecognizable from what they once were.

There isn't much in the way of public information about Malcoum Tate from before he was diagnosed with schizophrenia, in 1977. Young Malcoum received high marks. He was good at, and enjoyed, reading; then he went crazy. One day his mother drove with him on Baltimore's Wilson Street, where Malcoum spotted a mailbox with "Wilson" written upon it. The skewed logic of this coincidence triggered him to escape from the car, break into the nearest house, and brutally beat the man he found inside. This outburst led to his first hospitalization of five.

The National Alliance on Mental Illness (NAMI) describes itself as "the nation's largest grassroots mental health organization dedicated to building better lives for the millions of Americans affected by mental illness." NAMI is also known in the community of mental health advocates as the first place that scared, and often desperate, families go to for support and validation.

On its website, a pop-up emerges with the headline "We Call It *the NAMI effect.*" The NAMI effect is described as such:

Every time you offer your hand to pick someone up.
Every time you share your strength and ability to persevere.
Every time you offer support and understanding to a family who is caring for a loved one.
The NAMI effect grows.
Hope starts with *you*.

It's unclear from this pop-up who the targeted "you" is supposed to be.

NAMI prides itself on its activism: "Each day, NAMI effectively shapes the national public policy landscape for people with mental illness and their families." Such shaping is described in a 2012 report: listed causes under "Legislation to Improve Mental Health Care in America" include the Helping Families in Mental Health Crisis Act of 2016 (HR 2646) and the Strengthening Mental Health in Our Communities Act of 2014 (HR 4574). "NAMI parents," as the advocacy jargon goes—the parents of a child or children with mental health issues who are involved in NAMI-sanctioned activism—showed up and spoke out at 2014 committee meetings regarding California's Assembly Bill No. 1421 (AB 1421).

Public comment at such meetings occurred in counties across California as each deliberated over whether to adopt AB 1421, created in 2002 to open the door for the benign-sounding "assisted outpatient treatment," also known as the "involuntary treatment of any person with a mental disorder who, as a result of the mental disorder, is a danger to others or to himself or herself, or is gravely disabled." AB 1421 "would [also] create an assisted outpatient treatment program for any person who is suffering from a mental disorder and meets certain criteria." Like the idea of the Strengthening Mental Health in Our Communities Act, AB 1421 appears, in many ways, unassailable: who wouldn't want to give help to people who need it?

And yet the debate over AB 1421, as I discovered in San Francisco, touched upon crucial issues of autonomy and civil liberties. The bill makes the assumption that people who display a certain level of mental disorder are no longer capable of choosing their own treatment, including medication, and therefore must be forced into doing so. Sartre claimed, "We are our choices," but what has a person become when it's assumed that said person is innately in-capable of choice?

The Exorcist was released in 1973, four years before Malcoum Tate was first hospitalized. Named the scariest film of all time by *Entertainment Weekly, The Exorcist* is described by Warner Bros. as a movie about "an innocent girl . . . inhabited by a terrifying entity, her mother's frantic resolve to save her . . . and two priests . . . who come together in a battle of ultimate evil."

The "innocent girl" is Regan (Linda Blair), who becomes pos-sessed by the "terrifying entity" after using a Ouija board; her mother is Chris (Ellen Burstyn), a busy actress who receives invita-tions to the White House and purposefully bustles across crowded film sets. We first meet Regan as she bounds on-screen, all blunt bangs and big eyes, to give her mother a kiss hello. How was her day? Well, she played a game in the backyard, there was a picnic, and she also saw a "beautiful gray horse." She emphasizes her role as a sweetly privileged, all-American girleen as she wheedles, "Oh, Mom, can't we get a horse?" Even her use of the doomed Ouija board smacks of whimsy: when she first uses it on-screen, with Chris by her side, she demonstrates the spirit's presence by asking, "Do you think my mom's pretty?"

Once possessed, Regan vanishes. She hits her doctor—her face seems plastic; her voice is an unrecognizable growl. "Keep away!" she screams. "The sow is mine! Fuck me!" Chris, frustrated by Dr. Klein's explanations of her daughter's behavior, demands, "What are you talking about, for Christ's sake? Did you see her or not? She's acting like a fucking out-of-her-mind psychotic or a split personality."

As is Chris's story in *The Exorcist*, Pauline and Lothell's narrative is one about being both terrified and consistently let down. Regan's doctor, a figure of authority and a source of hope, is useless. Malcoum

Tate was repeatedly released from jails and hospitals once he was determined by authorities to be "better," or "not a threat to himself or others." After a yearlong 1984 hospitalization in Baltimore, Malcom improved, but his condition regressed approximately two years later after he stopped taking his medication. According to Lothell, Malcom kicked down an apartment door one morning in the fall of 1988, causing the family to be evicted. In both stories of possession we have a sense of familial desperation, of not knowing what to do.

In searching for local NAMI members who advocated for AB 1421, I was put in touch with a woman whom I'll call Beth. A chatty, impassioned woman who asked to remain anonymous, Beth has been a NAMI member since the mid-'90s. Ask her to talk about mental health public policy, and she does so in the manner of someone who is both well informed and highly opinionated; her many thoughts about jails and 5150s (code for involuntary hospitalization) and the dramatic story of her own mentally ill family member come out in a rush of memorized statistics and mental health policies.

Beth's family member, an adult male, lives with schizoaffective disorder. In relating the development of his illness, she says of him, "He was an excellent student, and the following year, he started having these rage attacks." She tried to get him treatment. The mental health system, a mess of private facilities, hospitals, and HMO-limited therapy sessions, has hospitalized him over seventy times, says Beth, which has repeatedly put her into dire financial straits. She continues to fight for the laws that she believes would help him, including AB 1421: "If you have a history [like he does] . . . of when he's off medicine, of getting so manic, and so violent that nine times in one year he's called the police himself, saying, 'Please take me to the hospital, I want to kill [Beth],' then that person should be on medication, not after he kills me or himself."

I nod when I talk to Beth. I say "Yeah" a lot. I find myself thinking, How can anyone possibly argue a case against this woman, who has found herself in terrible circumstances as she tries to help someone she loves?

Lothell Tate explained on the stand, "I was just saying to myself this is the only thing I know to do, that we done asked people to help us and we done begged people to help us and nobody did anything, and I was scared that one day Malcoum was going to lose his mind and harm me and my daughter."

It is impossible for me not to feel sympathetic toward Beth; it's even impossible for me to feel completely antagonistic toward Lothell and Pauline, both of whom were found guilty at their trial after only one hour of jury deliberation. I hear the bewilderment in Beth's voice when she talks about how there are no options for long-term care—when I ask, "In San Francisco or everywhere?," she replies, "All over the nation. Unless you have enough money." To say that the options for family members with severely mentally ill, psychotic relatives are limited is a comical understatement. People like Beth go to NAMI because they feel that there's nowhere else to turn.

Family-to-Family is NAMI's signature course, developed in 1991 by psychologist Joyce Burland. The twelve-session course, which is now in its fifth edition and has had over three hundred thousand participants, addresses families' emotional and practical needs in dealing with their loved one's mental illness.

"One of our . . . fundamental beliefs and awareness is that it can be a traumatic event to have a diagnosis of a mental health condition," the organization's national director of education, training, and peer support center, Colleen Duewel, told me. "And what we do is provide that light at the end of the tunnel of recovery, and of 'You can do this' and 'You're not alone,' and 'You have the support and the tools and the skill set you need.'"

As she discussed the "traumatic" nature of receiving a mental health diagnosis, I realized that she was doing so in the context of the family members surrounding the person with a mental illness, and not in the context of people being diagnosed with mental illness; in the Family-to-Family documentation, NAMI specifically states that the program is based on "a trauma model of family healing." When I asked her if most people coming to Family-to-Family feel "desperate," she paused. Carefully, she replied that "a fairly universal feeling is feeling alone . . . How do I take care of me? How do I take care of my loved one? How do I find resources?" She uses the phrase "burden of care"—as in, Family-to-Family has been found to decrease the burden of care one feels because of having a mentally ill family member.

Considering NAMI's origins, it's not surprising that the organization's focus tends to veer toward the family members who support a person with mental illness, and not the person with mental illness. As Duewel puts it, NAMI began when a couple of "mothers sitting at their kitchen table said, 'We've learned our lesson the hard way. How can we share this with other people, so they don't have to go through what we did?'" As with organizations such as Mothers Against Drunk Driving (MADD), it was the grassroots power of mothers caring for their children that fueled NAMI's creation. Beth calls her group the "NAMI Mommies." Duewel emphasized that "one of the most profound things that people get from [NAMI] is a sense of 'I'm not alone.'"

For those living with mental illness, there are other options. Julian Plumadore, the manager of the antistigma speakers' bureau SOLVE (Sharing Our Lives, Voices, and Experiences), and former community advocate of the Mental Health Association of San Francisco, describes MHASF as a "peer-run, recovery-oriented organization." I know Plumadore because I've been a speaker for SOLVE since 2013, and have heard in his talks the way he understands his recovery. He describes his story as one in which he was targeted as the "identified patient." The term is based on research on family homeostasis, and describes a pattern of behavior in which a dysfunctional family identifies one of its members as mentally ill, though their symptoms are actually manifestations of the family's pathology.

"*If only I could have gotten my shit together, everybody else's lives would have been fine* was the message that I was getting constantly, and so I was responsible for other people's happiness," he said—a difficult situation for anyone, but particularly challenging for someone diagnosed with a severe mental illness.

Plumadore, following MHASF's official stance on AB 1421 and other such policies, is against forced treatment. He's civil about, but clearly in disagreement with, "NAMI parents." I don't think I've ever seen him in anything but a button-down shirt, tie, and slacks, which is a conscious choice on his part; it's what he wears to meetings like the AB 1421 hearings, where the visual difference between the pro— and anti–AB 1421 constituents is obvious. "The rooms were divided," he said. "They were visibly split in two, and the power imbalance in those rooms was tangible. On one side of the room you would have the people who basically hold the power in society. Generally white, upper-middle-class, well-dressed professional people, the family members; and then on the other side of the room, you'd have a much more diverse group, generally more dressed down. . . . And," he finished wryly, "you could see in the room who was actually having the mental health issues, and who were the people who were trying to get them committed, essentially."

He told me about one woman, a mother, whom he spoke to at

an AB 1421 hearing. She spoke to him about her forty-year-old son, who is "living at home with her 'where he belongs.'" According to her, she is "his only hope." He highlights both phrases with horror. "They're so afraid of something bad happening to [their loved ones] out on the street, or out in the rest of the world, or [their family members] can't take care of themselves, [so] they guard them and keep them home. And that situation becomes increasingly tense and frustrating for everyone involved."

Plumadore knows about these situations because he was one of those people. The people who support forcible treatment sometimes don't believe him when he talks about abusing substances, being homeless, or acting, as he describes, "in scary ways in public." He's better now, he tells me, because he was finally told that he himself knows better than anyone else what he needs. For him, that included harm-reduction techniques instead of involuntary rehabilitation, as well as estranging himself from his family. Because he could discern a method of recovery for himself, he believes that the issue of personal, bodily autonomy must take precedence. Plumadore says those with mental illness almost universally experience the effects of trauma when forced into treatment, and disagrees with "hurting someone in order to help them." "We have the ultimate decision about what we're going to allow into our bodies, what we're not, and the decisions that we make about our own lives," he said.

A key concept in the discussion of schizophrenia, psychotic disorders, and treatment is that of how far the possession goes—or, in psychiatric terms, the level of "insight" the individual is capable of. To have poor insight is to have a lack of awareness about one's own condition. A fundamental argument for forcible treatment is that unwell individuals simply don't understand that they're ill, and therefore lack the ability to decide for themselves whether to, for example, take the recommended medication. Whether a person diagnosed with severe mental illness will take medication is an issue that repeatedly comes up in communities personally affected by mental illness; psychiatrists use the pejorative term "medication noncompliant" to describe those patients who won't take recommended medications, no matter the reason for the patients' decision.

I asked Beth what she wishes people would better understand, or what they currently misunderstand, about psychotic disorders. "There's all this stuff about, 'Give people information and they'll seek help on their own,'" she said. "Somebody who has a mind that they cannot trust because it's been taken over by whatever chemicals are not allowing them to think straight needs help in getting care, and they might need to be forced into it. It's comparable to Alzheimer's. Not to say that people with paranoid schizophrenia are demented or stupid, but they lose the ability to make rational decisions."

The mind has been *taken over*. The mind has *lost the ability to make rational decisions*. There's someone in there, but it's not whoever it is we formerly believed it to be. Depression is often compared to diabetes—in other words, it's not your fault if you get it, and you'll be fine if you just take care of it. Schizophrenia, on the other hand, is compared to Alzheimer's—it's still not your fault if you get it, but there's no fixing it, and though you may not intend to be a burden, you'll still be one until you die.

I do have experience with the loss of autonomy that comes with involuntary treatment, as well as the loss of status that comes with being described as lacking a sense of my own illness: I was hospitalized against my will in 2002, 2003, and 2011, and the records from my first involuntary, inpatient psychiatric hospitalization stated that I had "poor insight."

It is hard to convey the horror of being involuntarily committed. First, there's the terrifying experience of forcibly being put in a small place from which you're not allowed to leave. You're also not allowed to know how long you'll be there, because no one knows how long you'll be there. You don't have the things that you love with you: your journal, the bracelet your grandmother gave you, your favorite socks. Your teddy bear. There are no computers. In the hospitals where I've stayed, the only phones allowed were the landlines, which could be used at certain times of day for a certain period, causing patients to jockey for position by the phones and to bicker over who'd been taking too long.

Sometimes, someone will be allowed to bring something you cherish to you during visiting hours, although this must take place after a nurse inspects the goods; a lot of the time, your possessions won't be permitted into the ward because they include a sharp point or a wire coil or a dangerous piece of cloth. You're not allowed to choose what you eat, and within the limited choices that do exist, you're forced to choose only between things that are disgusting. You are told when to sleep and when to wake up. If you spend too much time in your bedroom, it indicates that you're being antisocial; if you do sit in the common areas but don't interact with the other patients, you're probably depressed or overly inward or perhaps even catatonic. Humans might all be ciphers to one another, but people with mental illness are particularly opaque because of their broken brains. We cannot be trusted about anything, including our own experiences.

We do get a brief sense of Regan's internal life before she is possessed. Chris spends one scene raging down the hall from Regan, who is in the foreground and in another room; when Chris screams, "No, don't tell me to be calm, god damn it!," the camera lingers on Regan, who glumly sits herself down. In another scene, the camera lingers on Regan's frightened face as Chris investigates a banging in the attic. We don't know what happened inside of Malcoum, other than hearsay about some anguished confusion over his mental state, or even what he was reported to have said when the shooting began, which was "Whatcha doing? Whatcha doing?" Instead, we see the nightmares that need to be solved. We see the possessions that have subsumed the sweet girl or the bookish boy, who are understood to be long gone. In the stories of who they were before the illness, or the evil, or the possession—including that of Beth's family member—there is an expectation of not only normalcy but goodness.

When I try to say that Solomon is incorrect when he speaks of the "likely reality" of schizophrenia as deletion, I recognize that it sounds like a form of denial. In speaking to a friend about the theory, she suggested that I might simply be parsing an inaccuracy: "How do they know?" she asked. And, more to the point, "Is everyone the same as they were ten years ago?" Of course, the fact that I don't listen to Yo La Tengo anymore isn't the same as fully believing, as I have done, that there are cameras installed in my shower. It's not the same as hallucinating, in daylight, a maggot-ridden corpse in a car. Yet I recognize the ability to make a choice: to reject an image or perception of what my experience of schizophrenia looks like. As far as I can tell, it does not look like Malcoum Tate's experience, whatever that actually was. I won't permit myself the audacity of presumption; but I particularly can't presume the experience of someone whose complicated humanity is now accessible only through anecdotes of "the problem child," "the nightmare," the reason for which a sister shot her brother while her mother waited in the car.

Malcoum Tate's murder is an extreme example of what happens when a family caring for a relative with schizophrenia feels that they have run out of options—that they have become overwhelmed by a force larger than themselves. The burden of care becomes the burden that breaks people. On the stand, Lothell Tate described the crime itself as an act of love: "I said to Malcoum, I said, 'Malcoum, I love you, and I only want what's best for you, and I'm sorry,' and I shot him . . . And I told him again, 'Malcoum, I love you, and I'm sorry,' and I shot him again until he quit moving."

And yet jurors spent only a single hour deliberating before returning with the verdict: Lothell Tate was sentenced to life in prison; later, her mother was sentenced to ten years as an accessory, reduced to one year with five years' probation. Judge Don Rushing told Lothell, upon her sentencing, that the way she killed Malcoum "truly was horrible," and "as brutal and dispassionate a murder as I've had a chance to see as a trial judge."

Lothell appealed once locally and then to the South Carolina Supreme Court, where her appeal was denied in 1990; she appealed again in 1991, and her appeal was again dismissed; her last appeal was denied in 1992. With that final rejection, Lothell stopped her diabetes treatment, and she died in a South Carolina state prison in 1994. I can't speak to her now, but I do imagine what it was like to be her on the night she killed her brother. When I think about the murder, I think about how excessive thirteen shots is. I also think about how a man who loomed over your bed in the middle of the night, a man who claimed to be sent by God to kill your daughter, might seem like a man possessed by evil, and therefore capable of anything, including surviving multiple gunshot wounds—even if you once loved him, or still do.

High-Functioning

At midday I entered the Chinatown Mental Health Clinic's guarded front doors, wearing a careful expression as I clipped into the waiting room. Inside the tiny space sat an elderly Chinese couple on a bench. The woman was clutching her head, and I considered how it takes so much—too much—energy to act as though our addled minds are all right. Few of the psychiatric facilities I've stayed in house those with the luxury for such performances. I was reluctant to stare, but felt monstrous for turning away from her pain, which was exactly what I did when I approached the partition and stated my purpose through the porthole to the woman behind the glass: "I'm a member of the local speakers' bureau, and I'm here to tell my story."

To the clinic I wore a brown silk Marc Jacobs dress with long sleeves, carefully folded up to the elbows. Buttons up to the dip between my collarbones, finished with a tied bow. No jewelry, save for a silver bangle and my wedding ring. Black wedge heels. Flat scars crisscrossed my bare ankles like dirt tracks. I wore an organic facial moisturizer that smelled like bananas and almonds, Chanel's

Vitalumière Hydra foundation in 20 Beige (discontinued), and a nubby Tom Ford lipstick in Narcotic Rouge (also discontinued, replaced by the inferior Cherry Lush).

My makeup routine is minimal and consistent. I can dress and daub when psychotic and when not psychotic. I do it with zeal when manic. If I'm depressed, I skip everything but the lipstick. If I skip the lipstick, that means I haven't even made it to the bathroom mirror.

In 2017, every morning I take a small and chalky pink pill; every night I take one and a half of the same pill. Haloperidol is, Dr. M reasons, what has kept me functioning without either delusions or hallucinations for the last four years, though for most of 2013 I struggled with what Sylvia Nasar, in *A Beautiful Mind*, calls schizophrenia's "dislocation of every faculty, of time, space, and body."

My official diagnosis didn't change to schizoaffective disorder for years. The disorder had been suspected, but not recorded, because schizoaffective disorder has a gloomier prognosis and more intense stigma than bipolar disorder does, and even psychiatrists can be swayed by the perceived severity of a different *DSM* code. Psychiatry also operates by treating symptoms and not a root cause, and so my psychopharmacological treatment was not impacted by the dramatic change in my chart. In *Blue Nights*, Joan Didion remarks, "I have not yet seen that case in which a 'diagnosis' led to a 'cure,' or in fact to any outcome other than a confirmed, and therefore an enforced, debility." My new diagnosis bore no curative function, but it did imply that to be high-functioning would be difficult, if not impossible, for me.

My talk for the Chinatown clinic was one that I adjusted for a variety of audiences: students, patients, doctors. It began with this line:

"It was winter in my sophomore year at a prestigious university." That phrase, "prestigious university," was there to underscore my kempt hair, the silk dress, my makeup, the dignified shoes. It said, *What I am about to disclose to you comes with a disclaimer.* I didn't want my audience to forget that disclaimer when I began to talk about believing, for months at a time, that everyone I love is a robot. "Prestigious university" acts as a signifier of worth.

Other signifiers: my wedding ring, a referent to the sixteen-year relationship I've managed to keep; descriptions of my treatment plan as if it were a stable, infallible Rosetta stone, when in fact the plan constantly changes in response to my ever-changing brain chemistry; the mention of the small online business, based on digital products and freelance work, that I started in early 2014. With these signifiers, I am trying to say that I am a wife, I am a good patient, I am an entrepreneur. I am also schizoaffective, living with schizoaffective disorder, living with mental illness, living with mental health challenges, crazy, insane—but *I am just like you.*

Whom "you" refers to depends on which talk I am giving. One of the clinic's group leaders, Henry, told me that I'd first be speaking to an audience of "high-functioning schizophrenics." Most of them, he told me, had been meeting there every week for ten years. I couldn't tell if this was said with pride as he guided me into the small meeting room.

There were fewer than ten people inside, not including Patricia, the head of the speakers' bureau. Almost all of them were, like I am, Chinese, save for one elderly white woman whose eyes cast about the room like hyperactive Ping-Pong balls. Before the talk began, Henry passed around photographs from a field trip. No one handed the photographs to me, the outsider. Without seeing the snapshots, I could only guess at the destination of a field trip for "high-functioning schizophrenics": maybe city hall, or perhaps a jaunt to

Muir Woods. The group quietly admired the photographs. Some of them spoke with the lilting disorganization that I associate with people who live relatively well with schizophrenia, given that they were spending time at the clinic—but who would immediately be labeled by many as crazy, to be pitied and even avoided.

Before the presentation began, Henry brought out a party-sized bag of Lay's. He searched the corners of the room for napkins and paper plates as a handsome twentysomething pried open the bag with his big hands. Nobody seemed terribly interested in engaging with me, and I was too busy reviewing my papers for this, my first talk in a clinical setting, to initiate contact. Patricia introduced the presentation by briefly speaking about the different kinds of stigma. A few people interrupted her with meandering commentary and needed to be gently rerouted by Patricia or Henry. The quiet ones avoided eye contact and said nothing.

With this group, I deviated from my script. When I told the story of my diagnosis and recovery, I exchanged complex language for simpler terminology. I removed the term "avolition." I leaned into descriptions of experiences that I thought they'd understand— including, in Mandarin, my mother's explanation for why she lied to my first psychiatrist about our family history of mental illness: "We don't talk about these things." In the final moments, I quoted from an email she sent after I resigned from my full-time editing position, having realized that the job was triggering psychotic episodes: "Fly free. I love you." The talk was designed to be inspiring. I was trying to *light up* the room with hope.

When I finished, two people were crying. Patricia, tear-streaked, showed me her arm: goose bumps. "I thought I had it bad," said the other woman who was crying, and my heart stammered in my chest. I *was* her, but I didn't want to *be* her. I was the one at the head of the table, visiting. She was the one who had come to this clinic every week for the last decade. Not much was changing for her—but everything, I had to believe, was possible for me.

During my first inpatient experience at a psychiatric hospital, I met two patients who were treated as markedly different from the rest of us: Jane and Laura. Jane was middle-aged and chatty; Laura was the only other Asian person on the ward, and spoke to no one. We patients rarely spoke of our diagnoses—at the time, I was diagnosed with bipolar disorder, with traits of borderline personality disorder—but everyone knew that Jane and Laura were the two with schizophrenia.

Jane was friendly, and frequently rolled up in her wheelchair to share disjointed monologues about the psychiatrists' "mind control experiments," ramblings paranoid enough to be considered psychotic, yet realistic enough to be unsettling to my vulnerable mind. In less coherent periods, her stories dissolved into the verbal nonsense known as "word salad," in which one word only tenuously relates to the one that came before it, and the assortment of them means nothing at all. These problems with communication caused her to be excluded, by doctors' decree, from otherwise mandatory group therapy sessions.

I never interacted with Laura, but I remember her yelling as she was pulled out of the hall bathroom, interrupted during an attempt to vomit up her medications. "They're poison!" she screamed as two nurses yanked at her long, skinny arms. "They're trying to poison me! They're trying to kill me!"

A natural hierarchy arose in the hospital, guided by both our own sense of functionality and the level of functionality perceived by the doctors, nurses, and social workers who treated us. Depressives, who constituted most of the ward's population, sat at the top of the chain, even if they were receiving electroconvulsive therapy. Because we were in the Yale Psychiatric Institute (now the Yale New Haven

Psychiatric Hospital), many of those hospitalized were Yalies, and therefore considered bright people who'd simply wound up in bad situations. We had already proved ourselves capable of being high-functioning, and thus contained potential if only we could be steered onto the right track. In the middle of the hierarchy were those with anorexia and bipolar disorder. I was in this group, and was perhaps even ranked as highly as the depressives, because I came from Yale. The patients with schizophrenia landed at the bottom—excluded from group therapy, seen as lunatic and raving, and incapable of fitting into the requirements of normalcy.

High-functioning patients had the respect of the nurses, and sometimes even the doctors. A nurse who respected me would use a different cadence; she would speak to me with human understanding. One gave me advice, saying that I needed to "dye my hair back"—it was clownishly red at the time—and "get down to normal living." As condescending as such words seem to me now, they were more than what was offered to those like Jane and Laura, who received only basic care. Forget about life advice—there was no hope for them beyond low-grade stability. Expectations are often low to begin with; in *A Beautiful Mind*, Nasar remarks that "unlike manic-depression, paranoid schizophrenia rarely allows sufferers to return, even for a limited period, to their premorbid level of achievement, so it is believed."

The psychiatric hierarchy decrees who can and cannot be high-functioning and "gifted." A much-liked meme on Facebook once circulated on my feed, in which a chart listed so-called advantages to various mental illnesses. Depression bestows sensitivity and empathy; attention-deficit/hyperactivity disorder allows people to hold large amounts of information at once; anxiety creates useful caution. I knew immediately that schizophrenia wouldn't make an appearance. Creative genius is associated with madness, but such genius, as explored in Kay Redfield Jamison's *Touched with Fire*, is primarily linked to depression or bipolar disorder. An exception is outsider artist Henry Darger, whose influential 15,145-page work *In the Realms of the Unreal* is both brilliant and the work of an obsessive, troubled mind that may or may not have been afflicted with schizophrenia—either way, Darger's inability to function in "normal" life is inextricable from his art.

With such unpleasant associations tied to the schizophrenias, it is no wonder that I cling to the concept of being high-functioning. As in most marginalized groups, there are those who are considered more socially appropriate than others, and who therefore distance themselves from those so-called inappropriate people, in part because being perceived as incapable of success causes a desire to distance oneself from other, similarly marginalized people who are thought to be even less capable of success.

An example of such distancing can be seen in Jenny Lawson's book *Furiously Happy: A Funny Book about Horrible Things*, which is often recommended to me as a hilarious memoir that embraces those with mental illness. Lawson, the beloved blogger behind *The Bloggess*, has been diagnosed with a variety of disorders, including depression and avoidant personality disorder. Yet she explains early in *Furiously Happy* that she is on antipsychotics—not because she is psychotic, she assures us, but because it decreases the length of her depressive episodes. "There is nothing better than hearing that there is a drug that will fix a terrible problem," she writes, "unless you also hear that the drug is for treating schizophrenia (or possibly that it kills fairies every time you take it)." But that line distressed me: for Lawson, my psychiatric condition, and the medications I take for it, put me on par with a fairy-killer; but if I were taking Haldol as a "side dish" for depression, I'd remain on the proper side of the mentally unwell.

Lawson, I'd like to believe, is trying to be honest rather than mean-spirited. Schizophrenia and its ilk are not seen by society as conditions that coexist with the potential for being high-functioning, and are therefore terrifying. No one wants to be crazy, least of all truly crazy—as in psychotic. Schizophrenics are seen as some of the most dysfunctional members of society: we are homeless, we are inscrutable, and we are murderers. The only times I see schizophrenia mentioned in the news are in the context of violence, as in *Newsweek*'s June 2015 opinion piece titled "Charleston Massacre: Mental Illness Common Thread for Mass Shootings." In this article by Matthew Lysiak, psychosis is linked to mass shooters such as Jiverly Wong, Nidal Hasan, Jared Loughner, and James Holmes. In the paragraph on Holmes, his treating psychiatrist is described as having written—and here I imagine a voice dripping with doom—that Holmes "may be shifting insidiously into a frank psychotic disorder such as schizophrenia." Immediately following that line, the piece reads, "On July 20, 2012 Holmes walked into an Aurora, Colorado movie theater and killed 12 people, injuring 70 others."

In a 2008 paper, Elyn R. Saks recalls, "When I was examined for readmission to Yale Law School, the psychiatrist suggested I might spend a year working at a low-level job, perhaps in fast food, which would allow me to consolidate my gains so that I could do better when I was readmitted." While fighting with my insurance company over disability benefits, I tried to explain that I can't work at McDonald's, but I can run a business based on freelance work. Place me in a high-stress environment with no ability to control my surroundings or my schedule, and I will rapidly begin to decompensate. Being able to work for myself, while still challenging, allows for greater flexibility in my schedule, and exerts less pressure on my mind. Like Saks, I am high-functioning, but I'm a high-functioning person with an unpredictable and low-functioning illness. I may not be the "appropriate" type of crazy. Sometimes, my mind does fracture, leaving me frightened of poison in my tea or corpses in the parking lot. But then it reassembles, and I am once again a recognizable self.

A therapist told me in my midtwenties, when my diagnosis was still bipolar disorder, that I was her only client who could hold down a full-time job. Among psychiatric researchers, having a job is considered one of the major characteristics of being a high-functioning person. Most recently, Saks has spearheaded one of the largest extant studies about the nature of high-functioning schizophrenia. In it, employment remains the primary marker of someone who is high-functioning, as having a job is the most reliable sign that you can pass in the world as normal. Most critically, a capitalist society values productivity in its citizens above all else, and those with severe mental illness are much less likely to be productive in ways considered valuable: by adding to the cycle of production and profit. Our society demands what Chinese poet Chuang Tzu (370–287 BCE) describes in his poem "Active Life":

Produce! Get results! Make money! Make friends! Make changes!
Or you will die of despair.

Because I am capable of achievement, I find myself uncomfortable around those who are visibly psychotic and audibly disorganized. I'm uncomfortable because I don't want to be lumped in with the screaming man on the bus, or the woman who claims that she's the reincarnation of God. I'm uncomfortably uncomfortable because I know that these are my people in ways that those who have never experienced psychosis can't understand, and to shun them is to shun a large part of myself. In my mind, there is a line between me and those like Jane and Laura; to others, that line is thin, or so negligible as not to be a line at all.

When asked, "What do people who live successfully with schizophrenia have in common?" for an awareness-raising social media campaign, Dr. Ashish Bhatt answered, "Often those persons who live successfully with schizophrenia are ones who have positive prognostic factors, which include good premorbid functioning, later age of symptom onset, sudden symptom onset, higher education, good support system, early diagnosis and treatment, medication adherence, and longer periods of minimal or absent symptoms between episodes."

Some of these factors and characteristics are determined by fate; others, however, have proved to be susceptible to human intervention, giving many people with schizophrenia—particularly young ones—a better chance to live high-functioning lives. In 2008, the National Institute of Mental Health launched a research initiative called RAISE (Recovery After an Initial Schizophrenia Episode), designed to explore the efficacy of certain kinds of early-intervention treatments. These types of treatments, known as Coordinated Specialty Care (CSC) treatments and supports, comprise a combination of tools, including case management, medication and primary care, cognitive-behavioral therapy, family education and assistance, and supported employment and education. Introducing this holistic approach to treatment takes into account a greater variety of factors that improve the odds for recovery. And, unlike in many other types of first-episode psychosis intervention, clients are encouraged to help guide their own treatment—thus contributing to higher rates of compliance and a greater sense of autonomy. Feeling some degree of control over their lives is particularly important for a population of people who are vulnerable to having none. As Dr. Lisa Dixon, director of OnTrackNY, told the *New York Times*, "We wanted to reinvent treatment so that it was something people actually want."

After the RAISE initiative determined that CSC treatment improved outcomes for people in the early stages of schizophrenia, early psychosis intervention programs began to appear around the country. As of 2016, such programs existed in thirty-seven states. At Stanford, the Prodrome and Early Psychosis Program Network started in 2014; in San Francisco, where I live, the Prevention and Recovery in Early Psychosis Network also addresses first-episode psychosis. Many provide services free of charge.

"Yet you *look* very put-together," Dr. M told me. I'd told her that, as a part of therapy, I was working on improving my hygiene. Showering became a challenge shortly after I began to hallucinate in college; my first experience with hearing voices occurred when a phantasm in the dorm showers intoned, "I hate you." This might have unnerved me enough to make me anxious about showering forever after. But because I care about my appearance, because I used to be a fashion blogger and writer, because I worked, for a time, at a fashion magazine and then as a fashion editor at a start-up company, I pass for normal more easily than do my comrades in the schizophrenias. When I browse the virtual aisles of La Garçonne, I am considering a uniform for a battle with multiple fronts. If schizophrenia is the domain of the slovenly, I stand outside of its boundaries as a straight-backed ingenue, and there is no telltale smearing beyond the borders of my mouth.

To some degree, the brilliant facade of a good face and a good outfit protects me. My sickness is rarely obvious. I don't have to tell new people in my life about it unless I want to. Although I no longer fret about when to disclose my psychiatric condition, I'm still aware of the shift that occurs when it happens. At a writers' residency, one woman responded to my disclosure with "I'm surprised to hear that. You don't seem to have those . . . tics and things." I reflexively smiled at this backhanded compliment. I suspect that she found comfort in being able to place me in a category separate from my brethren whose limbs and faces jerk from tardive dyskinesia, a horrific side effect of antipsychotic use that remains even if the medication is stopped. At a literary party, a wealthy patron who knew of my diagnosis told me that I should be proud of how coherent I am. In both anecdotes, I thanked the well-meaning women involved.

There are shifts according to any bit of information I dole out. Some are slight. Some tilt the ground we stand on. I can talk about the fact that I went to Yale and Stanford; that my parents are Taiwanese immigrants; that I was born in the Midwest and raised in California; that I am a writer. If the conversation winds its way to my diagnosis, I emphasize my normalcy. See my ordinary, even superlative appearance! Witness the fact that I am articulate. Rewind our interaction and see if you can spot cracks in the facade. See if you can, in sifting through your memory, find hints of insanity to make sense of what I've said about who I am. After all, what kind of lunatic has a fashionable pixie cut, wears red lipstick, dresses in pencil skirts and tucked-in silk blouses? What sort of psychotic wears Loeffler Randall heels without tottering?

My trajectory as a fashion writer began in 2007 with a blog called *Fashion for Writers* (*FFW*). At the time, big-name bloggers such as Susie Bubble, a.k.a. Susanna Lau, were developing cachet with the *Devil Wears Prada* old guard—Susie once even included *FFW* in her "blog roll" of links—which seemed to gesture toward the democratization of a historically elite industry. I could not afford the high-end stylings of Jane Aldridge, the wealthy Texan behind *Sea of Shoes*, but I had enough pocket money for 1930s dresses from Etsy and an enormous white faux-fur coat that earned me the nickname "Abominable Snowman" in graduate school. The oldest *FFW* posts, created while I was still a lab manager, mixed inane style commentary (e.g., pontificating on the return of pussy-bow secretary blouses) and clumsy "outfit of the day" photos taken with my digital camera propped up on books and, eventually, locked onto a cheap tripod.

In graduate school I invited a college friend, fellow writer and clotheshorse Jenny Zhang, to join *FFW*. We were both Chinese American, twentysomething women working to get our MFAs in blindingly white Midwestern towns, and Jenny, who had majored in ethnic studies, aimed the blog in a more political, and more interesting, direction. Eventually, Jenny took over *FFW* entirely before ending it in favor of greener pastures. Meanwhile, I moved on to work at a dubiously operated fashion and lifestyle magazine before settling in at a start-up that sold and produced vintage-inspired fashion, where I honed my copywriting chops and editing skills as I finished my debut novel. I sank my discretionary income from the start-up job into vintage, ultrafeminine silk chiffon and georgette and organdy dresses the color of candy floss, adorned with bows and tied up with satin ribbons; for a while, my Twitter profile read, "Taiwanese American. Weaponized glamour," the latter being a reference to Chaédria LaBouvier's work on the concept of "using beauty and style in direct, political ways that subvert dehumanizing expectations." Her thoughts on weaponized glamour are perhaps best known in her writing about Chimamanda Ngozi Adichie; Adichie, as a black woman author who writes about politics, who is dark-skinned and a feminist, is not an expected model of beauty to some, but is defiantly glamorous nonetheless.

I went to the Alexander McQueen exhibit *Savage Beauty* at the Met in 2011 because it was a significant occasion for people in the fashion industry, however peripheral. *Savage Beauty* reflected art as madness, darkness, beauty, death. McQueen's 2010 suicide hung over everything, throwing long shadows on the walls and the dresses. He'd ended his life not long after the death of his mother, and then the death of his friend Isabella Blow.

The piece that most beguiled and frightened me was a blank-faced, pure-white mannequin in a suit of inky feathers. In this ensemble, plumage forms massive shoulders that could be wings; the body displays a nipped, severe waist. There is nothing charming about this aviary costume. Encounter this creature in the shadows, and death has surely come to claim you. McQueen said about his clothing, "I want to empower women. I want people to be afraid of the women I dress," which is another truth about fashioning normalcy: the way I clothe myself is not merely camouflage. It is an intimidation tactic, as with the porcupine who shows its quills, or the owl that puffs its body in a defensive offensive: *dress like everyone should be terrified of you.*

And yet there are things that good costuming can't hide. For one season, I saw shadowy demons darting at me from all angles, and I couldn't control my response, which was to jump to the side or duck or startle at things that no one else could see. If I was with someone, I'd pretend afterward that nothing had happened, and usually my companion or companions who knew of my diagnosis would generously pretend that I hadn't just ducked, rather dramatically, for no reason. But I was mortified. It didn't matter how pulled-together I seemed when I was dodging specters that no one else could see. I knew that I looked crazy, and that no amount of snappy dressing could conceal the dodging. Because such movements were a necessary concession to my craziness, I responded by trying even harder to seem normal when I wasn't being assailed by hallucinations. I went dancing. I drank Jameson on the rocks and ate potato skins in Irish bars and pizza joints. I did all the normal things I could think of.

At the Chinatown clinic, I was led downstairs into a different room to give a second talk. This one was brighter, cleaner, and clearly the clinicians' domain. A water cooler stood burbling in one corner. The tables had been moved to flank the walls, allowing space for an assembly of folding chairs in the middle. The clinicians begin to wander in—men and women in business casual who found seats and stared into the middle distance. There was one man who sat in the back and actively scowled; his face read, *I can't believe I have to come to this goddamn thing.* He made me nervous, but it was also true that all of them, even the friendly-seeming ones, made me nervous.

Being faced with this many clinicians took me back to my first psychiatric hospitalization, when a battalion of psychiatrists, social workers, and psychologists made their daily rounds throughout the unit to interrogate us about how we were doing. The flock of officious questioners stopped by when I was sitting on the threadbare sofa near the television, or listlessly pushing around puzzle pieces at a table. Rarely did I experience such a radical and visceral imbalance of power as I did as a psychiatric inpatient amid clinicians who knew me only as illness in human form. During that first hospitalization, I learned that clinicians control when inpatients are granted privileges, such as being able to go downstairs for meals or outside to smoke for ten minutes twice a day. Most important, it was my team of clinicians who decided when I could go home. I became accustomed to playacting for the benefit of doctors: *Look! I'm happy! I'm fine!* In response to "Are you thinking about hurting yourself or others?" there was only one proper answer, which, regardless of what I said, was always followed by suspicious, persistent questioning. Knowing that it was time for me to talk about being crazy in front of a group of such people, even as a free woman, ratcheted up the rhythm of my already frantic heart.

When it was my turn to speak, I tried to sound eloquent. I slid "avolition" back into the talk. I emphasized, again, my education. I played up the entrepreneurship, mentioning the digital products I'd built and the clients I'd worked with. I added an extra bit of information about my time as a lab manager, when I was the head of a multisite study about bipolar disorder, and made weekly visits to the Stanford Department of Psychology's respected Bipolar Disorders Clinic as a researcher and not as a patient. The Bipolar Disorders Clinic is one of the best of its kind in the country, and I briefly wondered if these clinicians would even be able to find work there, which was a defensive and sour thought. All this posturing reads as paranoia, and even unkindness, toward the professionals who came to the clinic, who were not making as much money as, say, a psychiatrist at the Bipolar Disorders Clinic, and who did this good work because they'd been called to do it.

I finished my talk. No one was crying. The scowling man was still scowling, but less aggressively so.

As I sank back into my folding chair, Patricia asked if there were any comments or questions. A bespectacled woman raised her hand. She said that she was grateful for this reminder that her patients are human too. She starts out with such hope, she said, every time a new patient comes—and then they relapse and return, relapse and return. The clients, or patients, exhibit their illness in ways that prevent them from seeming like people who can dream, or like people who can have others dream for them. When she said this, I was fingering the skirt of my exquisite dress. I'd fooled her, or convinced her. Either way, I knew, was a victory.

Yale Will Not Save You

The moment I received my acceptance letter from Yale University was one of the happiest of my life. I stood at the bottom of my driveway, where two tin mailboxes nestled against one another, and found a large envelope waiting inside. Large envelopes from publications were a bad sign; they almost always bore my own handwriting, and usually held a rejected manuscript and a perfunctory note. But a big envelope from a university—an envelope with instructions, with welcome, with a full-color look-book—*that* was news. I stood at the mailboxes, shrieking. I was not the type of girl to shriek, but I was seventeen, and I had gotten into Yale. I was to be in Jonathan Edwards College, Class of 2005.

I was an overachieving child, the Michigan-born daughter of twenty-something Taiwanese immigrants who came to California with their baby girl. My parents were broke. They applied for food stamps; they told one another that someday they'd be rich enough to eat at Pizza Hut anytime they wanted. Eventually we moved for the sake of a different school district, and while raising me and my baby brother in a largely white small town, my parents told me that school was all-important and that I should always do my best. In elementary school, I assigned myself essays to write while on vacation. In fifth grade, I wrote a two-hundred-page novel about a kidnapped girl who becomes a cat. Soon my parents were both working in tech jobs at the height of the boom in Silicon Valley, and were no longer broke. They never spoke the words "American dream," but that was what their lives signified, and so in middle school I chose to take a 7:30 a.m. class in C++ programming, and I wrote a short story that my English teacher went on to teach even four years after that. In high school, when I told my mother that I was thinking of suicide, she suggested that we kill ourselves together, which I didn't fully recognize as the bizarre response it was until I told the story again and again over the following decades of my life. I won a gold medal at the Physics Olympics, was a California Arts Scholar, and crossed the stage at graduation with a GPA that belied the hundreds of self-inflicted scars lurking beneath my nylon gown. I chose to go east for college because I wanted to get away from the chaos—the accusatory fights, the sobbing—that occurred inside our home too often to take note of them.

I dated someone briefly at the end of my senior year of high school who broke up with me because I was undiagnosed and frightening, but before he ended our relationship he invited me to a poolside barbecue. He wore girls' jeans. We stood around the glassy pool at his apartment complex and his mother asked me what I was doing after graduation.

"I'm going to Yale," I said.

She did a double take. "Good for you," she said. Even back then my instability was clear to most.

"I went to Yale" is shorthand for *I have schizoaffective disorder, but I'm not worthless.*

Yale is the third-oldest university in the country, after Harvard, which is the oldest, and after the College of William and Mary, which was established in 1693. Yale used to be called the Collegiate School, but was renamed for Elihu Yale after a succession of gifts from the English merchant and philanthropist, including books, exotic textiles, and a portrait of George I. These generous donations, the sale of which helped to fund the construction of Yale College in New Haven, were vigorously encouraged by Puritan minister Cotton Mather, who also vigorously encouraged the Salem Witch Trials. In troubled Salem, babbling and odd movements could signify witchcraft. The bewitched Goodwin family children, he said, "would bark at one another like Dogs, and again purr like so many Cats." We all know what happened to the witches.

I was diagnosed with bipolar disorder the summer before I left for New Haven, the summer before the spring I was first hospitalized at Yale Psychiatric Institute (YPI). My then psychiatrist informed my mother and me that I had bipolar disorder. This diagnosis was the culmination of a month in which I demonstrated most of the classic signs of mania, including a hectic manner of speech and an uncharacteristic affair with a man eleven years my senior. Although the new diagnosis meant I required different medications than the ones I had been taking for depression and anxiety, she said, she would not prescribe me those new medications while I was under her care. It would be better if I waited until arriving at college, where I could have a doctor there prescribe the appropriate pills; the presumption was that my future psychiatrist would be able to monitor me appropriately. (Later my mother would tell me that had she truly understood what the doctor was saying, she never would have let me move cross-country to attend Yale.)

When school started, I began to see a doctor at what was then called the Department of Mental Hygiene at Yale University Health Services. Stigma clouded the visits, but I quickly learned that I could pretend to be visiting the Gynecology Department, which was on the same floor. I would exit the elevator and wait a few beats for the doors to close behind me before finally turning right, where students kept their eyes on their textbooks, notebooks, or hands—on anything instead of one another; if we looked long enough, it was possible to recognize the instabilities lurking.

The Department of Mental Hygiene didn't believe in assigning students both a therapist and a psychiatrist, which would create the inconvenient need for back-and-forth communication, and so I saw a woman that year who served as both. She prescribed me Depakote, also known as valproate or valproic acid, which is an anticonvulsant used as a mood stabilizer. She returned again and again to the subject of my mother, whom she blamed for most of my emotional difficulties. During my first semester at Yale, my mother swelled and grew monstrous in my mind; she loomed as someone whose emotional lability had imprinted me with what I frankly called an inability to deal with day-to-day life.

Much of the time, I told the doctor, I felt too sensitive to cope. I was in constant agony. I liked my doctor well enough, but I didn't seem to be improving, and the skittish feeling beneath my skin warned of trouble. Eventually, I would stop sleeping for days at a time; then off I would go.

Yale introduced me to swooning over course descriptions in the Blue Book; "shopping period"; my being openly queer; life without my family, whom I avoided calling for months; WASPs; the attitudes and postures of Old Money; goat cheese; people who bought six-hundred-dollar boots; the understanding that six-hundred-dollar boots existed; legacy students who'd known the fight songs since birth; Gothic architecture; Beinecke Plaza; Audiogalaxy; theory; statistical analysis; a shy young man in ill-fitting jeans I met at a party, who would eventually become my husband; 9/11 and the War on Terror; Islamophobia; Wong Kar-Wai and *In the Mood for Love*; secret societies; falafel and lemonade; binge-drinking screwdrivers; Animal Models of Clinical Disorders; being offered, but never taking, cocaine; carillon bells ringing out Handel and "Hit Me Baby (One More Time)" as I walked to class, or stared out my dorm window; how to dress for snow; saying "I love you" and meaning it; eggnog in December; feeling so very special, as though virtuous, simply because of where I went to school.

Yale is mocked for its determination to be elite from the get-go—for fashioning itself in the likeness of Oxford and Cambridge, and then having acid dumped on itself to simulate age. Yale is, in the world of elite universities, a prepubescent girl swiping on mascara before the first day of middle school. Yale's campus is still the most beautiful campus I know.

Many of my classes, including Introduction to the Human Brain, took place in Linsly-Chittenden 102. Larger than a seminar room but smaller than a lecture hall, LC 102 is famous for an elaborate Tiffany window along one wall, titled *Education*. Art, Science, Religion, and Music are depicted as angels across its panes. The center section depicts Science surrounded by personifications of Devotion, Labor, Truth, Research, and Intuition.

(Why is Intuition the province of Science? Why is Inspiration governed by the angel of Religion, which is to the right of it, and not by the angel of Art?)

During a manic episode, I scribbled nonsense along the center and edges of my notebook pages, where I was ostensibly taking notes. The words crawled like spiders. *Look. The edge why position not under where? Lit light like night.* The center figure of *Education* was a trifecta of the things I wanted from my Ivy League schooling: Light—Love—Life.

In the elevator, among a group of acquaintances—other members of an Asian American performance art group I'd joined—the topic of the Mental Hygiene Department arose.

Someone's eyes widened. "Watch out for that place," she said.

"I have a friend who went there," someone else said. "He stopped because he knew they'd put him in [Yale Psychiatric Institute] if he kept talking."

"They'll put you in YPI for *anything*," the first person said.

"Never tell them you've thought about killing yourself," they counseled me. I was a freshman. They were taking me under their wing, offering me wisdom. "Never tell them you're thinking about killing yourself, okay?"

I think about that advice now: never tell your doctor that you're considering killing yourself. Yet this was sound advice, in the end, if I wanted to stay.

Margaret Holloway, known as "the Shakespeare Lady," hustled on campus by reciting Shakespeare for spare change. According to rumor, she'd once been a student at the esteemed Yale School of Drama, but had dropped out after a psychotic break. (In truth, she had graduated from the School of Drama in 1980, and experienced the first symptoms of schizophrenia in 1983.) Like most students, I'd heard that the Shakespeare Lady possessed encyclopedic knowledge.

I encountered the Shakespeare Lady only once. One night, my

then boyfriend, now husband, C., and I decided to pick up dinner at Gourmet Heaven, the bougie convenience store on Broadway that carried an astonishing variety of Haribo gummies. I'd never seen such thick fog in New Haven. Holloway appeared like something out of a dream: thin, and asking us for twenty dollars. She needed it to get into the women's shelter, she told us, and she wanted a specific brand of yogurt that she could get only at Gourmet Heaven, but she was banned from the store because of the corrupt police. I know now that in 2002 she was arrested for blocking the entrance of Gourmet Heaven, and apparently was arrested several times after that for other small crimes. In 2004, when I was no longer a student at Yale, she had gotten down to ninety pounds, and in 2009 she was in the local news for "cleaning up her act." On that foggy night, I gave her more money than she'd asked for, and waited with her while C. went to buy the yogurt she'd requested. I didn't ask her to recite Shakespeare.

In 2002, I asked my therapist-slash-psychiatrist—not the woman I'd originally been assigned, but a man who became my doctor after my first hospitalization, and who looked like Gene Wilder—"Are there any students here with schizophrenia?"

"Why do you ask?" he asked.

I didn't answer, but what I'd meant was: *Is there anyone here who's worse off than I am?*

The fog was still pressing its velvet paws to the windows when C. and I returned to his dorm that night. I rested my face against his shoulder, and he asked me what was wrong. I asked him if he thought I could become the Shakespeare Lady. If my mind might go so far it couldn't make its way back.

"It won't happen to you," he said, though I had asked a question that resisted reassurance, and I knew it. In truth, neither of us could know. Still, I needed to hear his promise that I would be okay.

I would ask him variations on this question over the next decade or so: "I'm not going to be crazy forever, am I?" But we never spoke of the Shakespeare Lady again.

Michelle Hammer did not go to Yale, but she was one of those mysterious college students with schizophrenia whom I tried to learn about through my Gene Wilder psychiatrist; I learned of her through the advocacy-focused clothing line she runs, called Schizophrenic.NYC. In high school, Michelle told me, she believed that her mother was trying to kill her; once she was accepted into college, where she would play lacrosse, she was relieved by the notion that she would be safe from harm. Within a few months at school, however, Michelle began to fear that her roommate was trying to kill her. It was at that point, she told me, that she came to a realization: "It's me; it's not everybody else. Why do I think this way?"

Michelle went to the student health center. She hoped to be diagnosed with something, because the idea of being "crazy" scared her, and the promise of treatment offered some kind of hope. After an initial evaluation, she was told she had bipolar disorder, and made an appointment with a psychiatrist, who prescribed Zoloft. "It didn't go well," she said. "[The psychiatrist] never told me that these medications can make you more depressed or more upset. So I would take it, [but] I would not take it; I would take it; I would not take it, and then . . . So that's all first semester going into the winter break."

It was during the winter that things got truly bad. There was a snowstorm, Michelle said, and classes were canceled. She was getting drunk in the dorm—a forbidden activity—when she began to become afraid: "I'm thinking, I'm gonna get in so much trouble. All the terrible stuff. I took a piece of glass and slit my wrist."

The girls down the hall found out. Someone from the university police department (UPD) showed up—"this six-foot-tall, humongous woman," Michelle said—and tried to figure out what was going on. Everyone, including Michelle, was shepherded into the dorm's common room.

"So everybody's in there," Michelle said, "and we're all in a semicircle around her . . . She goes, 'I heard there's a problem here. Everybody lift up your sleeves.' So pretty much she starts on the left, everybody's lifting up their sleeve and they're all good. And she gets to me, and I go, 'Yeah.' And then she goes, 'Well, I wanna see your arms.' And I go, 'Well, how about we just go into my room.' 'Cause this is about three feet away [from everybody else], and I could just show her in my room, 'cause it's very embarrassing to do that to anybody. Especially in front of all these people."

According to Michelle, she turned around to go into her bedroom—and the woman from UPD grabbed the hood of her sweatshirt and threw her onto the floor. Michelle tried to crawl under her desk. "All of a sudden," she said, "my neck gets stepped on with a huge boot. And she steps on me and she puts her pepper spray right in front of my face, and she says, 'Don't move or I'm gonna spray you.'" Finally, Michelle was handcuffed. Despite the woman's repeated questioning, she continued to refuse to pull up her sleeve—even as she was pinned up against a wall on the floor—even as she kicked her leg out and booted the UPD officer straight in the face. In the end, the officer took Michelle to a hospital.

It was clear, in hearing all of this, that Michelle remains resentful about how she was treated by the officer who came to assess the situation. Without prompting, Michelle gave me the full name of the woman. She said, "It took me about nine years to be able to tell that story." It isn't clear whether the officer was given crisis de-escalation training, or any kind of training at all in dealing with mentally ill students. I can easily picture the scenario: a campus cop goes into a dorm, knowing only that a student has cut her wrist. The dorm-mates are whipped into chaos because of alcohol and a snowstorm and the dramatic, self-destructive behavior of one of their own.

Periodic blood tests need to be taken when on Depakote, the medication I was prescribed when I arrived at Yale—not only to monitor the level in the blood, but also to check the health of my liver. I'd had my blood tested several times before the spring of 2002. No one had ever told me anything was wrong.

A few weeks before spring break, I started needing less sleep. Instead of growing tired at night, the day would crowd in on the empty space, demanding to be filled by activity. My thoughts skittered through like messages on ticker tape, and I wanted to run instead of walk; I punched a tree on Cross Campus, shuddering with an energy my body couldn't contain. The mania was at first a welcome change from the inexplicable fifteen hours of sleep I often needed each night. As most manic episodes do, however, the mania swiftly escaped my control—my thoughts rearranged themselves into nonsensical, violent shapes, and soon I stopped sleeping completely. If anyone noticed, they kept it to themselves, although C. was concerned and said so. I'd told him about my diagnosis of bipolar disorder, but bipolar disorder had no visceral corollary for him. He not only lacked the experience to know what the illness truly meant, but he also had no plan for what to do in a psychiatric emergency.

After the wild high came the low. My thoughts leaped to suicide—my entire life had been marked by illness and depression, and there was no reason to think that it wouldn't continue in the same way. I was convinced that I would be depressed forever, though the previous week alone had proved this belief to be erroneous. My vision remained myopic and dim as I wrote two lists in a notebook, marking down the pros and cons of permanently removing myself from my life. The cons list was longer than the list of pros, but I knew that I was in trouble.

Around this time, I received a phone call from the student health lab with the results of my blood work, which surprised me because they'd never called before. "Your liver looks fine," they said, "but did you know that you've never had a therapeutic level of Depakote in your blood?"

Upon hearing this, the clamor in my head soured, becoming what is known in mood disorder parlance as a "mixed episode." Such episodes occur when a person is experiencing symptoms of both a manic and a depressive phase, such as in episodes of agitated depression. It is considered a dangerous state to be in if that person is suicidal; a severely depressed person will find it hard to summon enough energy to plan and execute a suicide, but a severely depressed person shot through with norepinephrine is reckless enough to do both. My doctor, it seemed, had never adjusted my Depakote to a therapeutic dose while I was in her care. I couldn't get over the incompetence. If she couldn't be bothered, why should I bother to keep living when it was so hard to be alive? Suicide seemed like a good option, and yet I walked with my lists to the Mental Hygiene Department; despite the warnings I'd been given about expressing suicidal ideation to a Yale psychiatrist, I didn't actually want to die. At Mental Hygiene, I was assigned to Urgent Care, and when the psychiatrist on call heard about the lists, I was dispatched to YPI. I wasn't strapped down—I would be the next time, after taking an overdose—but I was placed in an ambulance. A nurse at Mental Hygiene reassured me that my doctor would meet me at the hospital. As it happened, she never came.

After over a week at YPI, I reached a compromise with the dean and the head of psychiatry: I could stay at Yale if my mother came to stay with me, off-campus, for the rest of the year. (Upon hearing of this plan, a friend who knew of my family history said, "I thought they wanted you to get *better*.")

My mother lived with me in a small two-bedroom apartment that was close to both my residential college and a stretch of loud bars. Slowly, our relationship improved, even if my illness didn't. Between classes I escaped to the bathtub; because hot water was scarce in the apartment, my mother carried in stockpots of hot water from the stove. She made Taiwanese noodle dishes. She wrote elaborate medication charts on watercolor paper. She called my psychiatrist when I lay writhing on the floor, sobbing, caught in knotty torment.

Somehow, I made it through that year. I had a summer away from Yale, at home in California, and then I went back in the fall, when the weather was still hot and damp like the inside of a feverish mouth. I was shaken, and wanted more than anything to be okay.

I'm still trying to figure out what "okay" is, particularly whether there exists a normal version of myself beneath the disorder, in the way a person with cancer is a healthy person first and foremost. In the language of cancer, people describe a thing that "invades" them so that they can then "battle" the cancer. No one ever says that a person *is* cancer, or that they have *become* cancer, but they do say that a person is manic-depressive or schizophrenic, once those illnesses have taken hold. In my peer education courses I was taught to say that I am a person with schizoaffective disorder. "Person-first language" suggests that there is a person in there somewhere without the delusions and the rambling and the catatonia.

But what if there isn't? What happens if I see my disordered mind as a fundamental part of who I am? It has, in fact, shaped the way I experience life. Should the question be a matter of percentages of my lifetime, I've spent enough of this lifetime with schizoaffective disorder to see it as a dominant force. And if it's true that

I think, therefore I am, perhaps the fact that my thoughts have been so heavily mottled with confusion means that those confused thoughts make up the gestalt of my self; this is why I use the word "schizophrenic," although many mental health advocates don't.

My friends with anxiety disorders, for example, tend to speak of anxiety as a component of their personalities. Laura Turner writes, in her essay "How Do You Inherit Anxiety?," "It is from Verna Lee Boatright Berg that I inherited my long face, my quick hands, my fear that someday soon I will do something wrong and the world will come to a sharp end." In their minds, there is no tabula rasa overlaid by a transparency of hypochondria, generalized anxiety disorder, or obsessive-compulsive disorder; such thoughts are hardwired into their minds, with no self that can be untangled from the pathology they experience. Another friend's obsessive-compulsive disorder has calmed significantly since she began taking Prozac, but she continues to be most comfortable when things are tidy, even though her tidiness is no longer disruptive. She still washes her hands more thoroughly than anyone I know.

There might be something comforting about the notion that there is, deep down, an impeccable self without disorder, and that if I try hard enough, I can reach that unblemished self.

But there may be no impeccable self to reach, and if I continue to struggle toward one, I might go mad in the pursuit.

I left Yale for good in early 2003, although I did not know at the time that it was the end. I'd been hospitalized for the second time at the institute—two times in one year, was the way the head of psychiatry put it, although it was two times in two school years—and because of this breach of etiquette, they asked me to leave.

The dean at my residential college gave me the choice of declaring my departure to be a voluntary medical leave. If I officially named it for what it was, he explained, an involuntary medical leave would be a black mark of which I could never rid myself. Offering me this choice was meant as a kindness, but I was unable to see anything that they did to me that month, including putting me in two-point restraints, as a kindness.

Yale told me to leave immediately. I was not allowed to reenter campus, and so someone confiscated my student ID, and my busy father, who had flown from China to be with me, was tasked with packing my things. I was told to be at JFK on the same night that I left the hospital—so urgent was Yale's desire for me to leave. But my father, in his largesse, instead arranged for C. and me to stay at the New Haven Hotel for a night. By then C. and I had been together for over a year; the next few years would be spent in a long-distance relationship, although at the time we had no idea how we'd manage to stay together. Upon my expulsion from Yale, we had one night to say good-bye.

While sitting in my father's hotel room, talking things over before leaving for ours, my father's phone rang. He answered it. It was someone from Yale. "Are you in New York?" they asked.

"Yes," he lied.

The only thing I remember from our night in that hotel is that I fell asleep early while C. watched *Showboat*. I would never return as a student again.

In 2014, Katie J. M. Baker published an article in *Newsweek* titled "How Colleges Flunk Mental Health." It was the piece I'd been waiting for—after blogging about my Yale experience, I'd received a flood of emails from students battling to stay in their colleges, students on enforced leave from their colleges, and former college students who, like me, were never allowed to return to school. In her article, Baker makes the case that psychiatric illness is punished by colleges and universities that instead ought to be accommodating students under the Americans with Disabilities Act (ADA). Rather than receiving help, mentally ill students are frequently, as I was, pressured into leaving—or ordered to leave—by the schools that once welcomed them. The underlying expectation is that a student must be mentally healthy to return to school, which is difficult and unlikely to happen to the degree the administration would like. This is saying, essentially, that students should not have severe mental illness.

How the ADA works for mentally ill students varies from school to school. I have no memory of Yale telling us anything about registering as a disabled student, though such an explanation might have happened. When I transferred to Stanford, in 2003, the Office of Accessible Education reached out to me in order to set up accommodations, which felt like a godsend. At the University of Michigan, where I received my MFA in fiction, it is possible to register a mental health condition as long as the diagnosed illness or disorder "substantially limits one or more major life activities." "It is important to note," the student life website states, "that a mental disorder in or of itself does not necessarily constitute a disability." Students seeking to register their disabling mental disorder must send a completed verification form, and if they qualify, they will be assigned a disability coordinator. This system is worlds better than it was when I researched disability accommodations for mentally ill students a handful of years before this writing. In 2009, I was also told during my graduate student instructor training to never give accommodations to students claiming to be depressed, because it was easy enough to pretend to be depressed.

Baker adroitly points to the difficulties colleges and universities face when it comes to dealing with students with mental health issues: institutions of higher education fear liability, because no school wants to be sued over a student's suicide, or held responsible for a mass shooting. According to many who live and work at them, colleges and universities can't realistically be expected to give students with severe mental illness the treatment they need.

What hope does exist for improved conditions rests in the hands of organizations such as the Office for Civil Rights, which is "actively developing policy" regarding best practices—although the progress of such policy development is opaque at best. The Saks Institute for Mental Health Law, Policy, and Ethics held a 2014 symposium called Many Voices, One Vision: Assisting College and University Students with Mental Illness Make the Most of Their Academic Experience, which included sessions on "reasonable accommodations" and "preventing fear, risk management, and miscommunication from derailing a successful academic experience." The Jed Foundation, a national nonprofit that describes itself as "[existing] to protect emotional health and prevent suicide for our nation's teens and young adults," announced in 2014 that fifty-five colleges are examining their health services, with a focus on mental health policies. A cursory online search, however, indicates that in higher education not much has changed for mentally ill students, who are still being regularly ejected for being too crazy for school.

In a 2014 article in the *Yale Daily News*, Rachel Williams describes her experience with an evaluating official at Yale who, after hearing that she cut herself, told her that she needed to go home. "'Well the truth is,' he says, 'we don't necessarily think you'll be safer at home. But we just can't have you here.'"

I went on a yearlong voluntary medical leave. I took classes at UC Berkeley and the California College of the Arts, and I worked as a web designer too. I dabbled in marketing. Always, I planned to go back to Yale, where C. was finishing his senior year. He was sane; he could still freely roam the campus and its outskirts. I made a list of things that I would do once I returned: go to more art shows, join clubs, make new friends. I concocted plans to live in an apartment off-campus with an avant-garde blond and a pothead friend who had a crush on me.

I flew to New Haven for four interviews that would determine whether I was fit to return. The only interview I remember is one in which a jolly man I'd never met told me I seemed ready to come back. I flew home to California and waited to hear back from them, and when I did, the answer was no.

From an email I sent to Yale University's head of psychiatry:

Dear Dr. X,

My mother and I left messages yesterday and today in hopes of reaching you, but we never heard back or received any hint of when we might possibly hear back. I thought I would try the email approach, although you are probably deluged with emails all of the time.

I was surprised (as were all of my friends, family, etc.) to hear that I had not been readmitted, even though I had tried to prepare myself for the worst. Dean C told me to call you, as you would have information on how to "make [my] application more viable the next time." If you do have such information, I would like to hear it. It frustrates me to know that I was not readmitted, because I have become quite certain in the past year that I am more than ready to return—my friends know this, my family knows this, and my doctors at home know this. Unfortunately, the litany of people who know that I am ready to return does not include the readmission committee. I am not sure why there is such a disparity of opinion, but I am hoping that you will be able to give me some idea through your knowledge of what makes a more viable application. I keep wondering what it is that I did wrong. Was it my grades? My essay? The recommendation letters? Was it something I said during the interview process? (Unfortunately, one of the interviewing deans even told me that he/she would give me "a glowing recommendation." I guess that glowing recommendation did not do much for me in the end.)

One statement that kept coming back to me during the interview process was that the committee was deciding not *whether* I could return to Yale, but rather *when*. I surmise that the committee has decided that it is in my best interests to keep me away from school for another semester, probably to "grow" or "mature"—I can't speak for them and you, obviously; I can only guess. And I know that I will have to, out of self-preservation, find interesting things to do during that semester. The disappointing part is that I know that this semester (and maybe even more semesters after that—the way the process looks to me right now, I can't fathom how these decisions are made or how they are swayed) will probably go by the same way this past year on medical leave has gone by: with me at the end feeling fine, excited to go back to school, and knowing that my fate is being judged based on how well I show off just how very fine I am.

I was also wondering why you never contacted my doctors at home, considering they know me very well and have worked with me during my leave, and also considering the fact that you told me you would at the end of the week I went to the interview.

I would like it very much if you could respond to my questions as much as possible, as this has been a few days of frustration and disappointment (with no end in sight) and it would help to understand the process behind what seems right now to be a very arbitrary and incorrect decision. Also, I am at a loss as to what to do this next semester. I do not think a school would allow me to register to take classes this close to spring semester. What is required of me if I want to reapply again?

As stated before, a response would be very much appreciated. Thank you for your time.

In the end, Yale owed me nothing, not even an explanation. It did not have to admit me a second time once I'd proved lunatic, nor does it have to acknowledge in its alumni magazines, all these years later, that I was ever a student; it does not have to allow me into the Yale Club in Manhattan.

And I owe Yale nothing. I recycle the donation requests C. receives without opening them. Same goes for the alumni magazines.

When I was a Yalie, I used to shoplift. Rarely did I take anything substantial: a pen here and there from the art store, a headband once from Urban Outfitters. One day I was holding a stack of books at the campus bookstore on Broadway and saw that the line was a long one. Impulsively, I held my head high and walked out of the store, still carrying the books. No alarms went off. No one chased me. I look back and tell myself that I was young and stupid; then I catch myself. One of the few photographs I have of myself from college is a snapshot of me standing in front of the Urban Outfitters on Broadway, holding up a sleeveless shirt I'd bought on sale. I have a big smile and chopped-off bangs. I am young and full of mistakes that I have yet to make, but I'm not the only one who erred back then.

The Choice of Children

In the spring of 2007, the clinical director of Camp Wish, who was also my coworker at the Stanford Department of Psychiatry, told me that my experience with clinical interviews made me an excellent potential volunteer for a youth bipolar camp. We were standing in front of the office elevator. I smiled and told her to send me an application, but I didn't tell her what I really thought.

As I stepped into the elevator, I envisioned seventy-two hours with nine-to-eighteen-year-old kids with bipolar disorder. They might be hallucinating. They might have multiple diagnoses, including Asperger's, attention-deficit disorder (ADD), attention-deficit/hyperactivity disorder (ADHD), pervasive developmental disorder (PDD), and oppositional defiant disorder (ODD). At their worst, they would be shouting, screaming, crying, and possibly violent. At their best, they would want to—here I gave an inward, cynical shudder—*play* with me.

At the time I believed that my alleged dislike for children was likely rooted in self-deception. I used to eat sweets, and after I decided to cut back on sugar for dietary reasons, I learned to say, in lieu of a more thorough explanation, "I don't like dessert." For years I didn't put sugar in my coffee; at times, I found fruit too saccharine. No one who met me during a particular decade knew that I had once gorged on cheesecake and caramels. Similarly, I avoided playing with children, because I was afraid of awakening a biological and emotional drive. I didn't say, *I don't like children*, but that's what I thought every time someone tried to hand me a baby.

Yet I couldn't get over the concept of sixty kids with the same diagnosis getting together to have a good time. To have bipolar disorder means that you might wrap your car around a tree in a manic frenzy, or spend your life savings on socks because you think the Ice Age is coming, or shoot yourself because the pain is just that bad, and very few people, except the estimated 1 to 2 percent of the population who share your diagnosis, will understand. Children with bipolar disorder may have a different form of the disorder than their grown-up counterparts, but their lot is just as bad, if not worse—according to the National Alliance on Mental Illness, "[Pediatric bipolar disorder] appears more severe and with a much longer road to recovery than is seen with adults." I wanted to help the kids at Camp Wish, but I turned in my application to Megan with an ulterior motive: I also wanted to feel less alone.

Camp Wish was established in 2005 as a "typical" summer camp for bipolar children and adolescents who would have problems in a standard sleep-away camp setting—these problems perhaps being one of the reasons that the camp lasts for only three days. The setting is bucolic, with rolling yellow hills and a smattering of trees. A family foundation donated its grounds to Camp Wish, and were you to happen upon the camp, you might overlook the signs of severe bipolar disorder in the assemblage of nine-to-eighteen-year-olds in favor of the sight of the plush cabins, expansive dining hall, and vast recreational areas filled with young people engaged in macramé and basketball.

Bipolar disorder has yet to be fully understood in adults, and it is even more mysterious in children. Those with pediatric bipolar disorder have less-distinguishable mood states that can fluctuate rapidly, making the illness difficult to diagnose. Is a child who acts out in class suffering from ADHD, ODD, a manic state, both, or neither? Other behaviors associated with pediatric bipolar disorder include hypersexuality, hallucinations and delusions, suicidal behavior, violence, agitation, and impaired judgment. The very existence of pediatric bipolar disorder is controversial among those who believe that children are too young to be diagnosed with such a weighty mental illness, or those who think that diagnoses such as ADHD and ODD, in combination with unipolar depression, also known as major depression, are more fitting labels for the kind of irritability and rage that often manifest in said children.

The foundation that sponsored Camp Wish believed that pediatric bipolar disorder is a real and terrible thing. Its website—touching upon a commonly referenced statistic—mentioned that it affects approximately two million children in the United States. C. and I went to camp with sixty of them in the summer of 2007.

Aaron was stocky with close-cropped blond hair. He liked football and rarely smiled. Julian frequently smiled and wore a green bandanna around his neck. Mark wore the same clothes every day: a white T-shirt, cargo shorts, and a backward baseball cap. He collected small things like toy planes and pebbles to put in his pockets. Alex looked a lot like Julian, except for the green bandanna. Stuart, the smallest of the five boys, was short, thin, and had his shirt perpetually tucked into his shorts, with tube socks pulled up as far as they could go.

As head counselor of our four-counselor, five-boy cabin, C. carried with him a massive blue binder filled with surveys. These surveys, painstakingly filled out by the boys' parents prior to coming to Camp Wish, covered the basics: comorbid (multiple) diagnoses, severity of bipolar disorder, food preferences, hospitalization history, medication regimen, and so forth. The surveys also covered smaller, though still essential, details. One boy could sleep at night only while listening to his iPod; all the boys had bed-wetting issues; they all enjoyed playing sports (which I dreaded). A question that I found particularly poignant in its frankness was "How do you and your child deal with the onset of rage or mania?"

For over a decade, I have not wanted, or even considered having, biological children, but these days I find myself frequently on the receiving end of unsurprising "news." Where once the announcement "We have news!" from a couple almost inevitably meant a marriage announcement, the statement is now followed, particularly if the couple is heterosexual, by "We're pregnant!"

Though those closest to me know exactly why I am not having children, and exactly why I am not considering adoption, either, I'm still asked by a healthy few if childbearing and/or child-rearing is part of my life plan. If I barely know the person, I say something vague about having a severe, genetic medical condition, and leave it at that. If pressed further, I talk about the medications that I take, their potential detriment to a fetus, the complications that are likely to ensue postpartum, and the genetic chances of passing my disorder on to my child.

And there is also the question posed to me by those who seemingly cannot bear the idea of my not having a child in my life: "But what about adoption?"

What I want to say is *I have schizoaffective disorder. I was psy-*

chotic for half of 2013, and I could be psychotic again at any moment. I don't want to put a child through having me as a mother. I am livid at the inquiry.

Once, I did want biological children. And then, hours after pausing in front of a children's clothing store in San Jose, California, I did not. It was early in my relationship with C., who was then still only a boyfriend, still in his early twenties. I watched women purchase tiny pea coats and miniature blouses with Peter Pan collars, with my own shopping bags hanging at my sides. Later I called him and said, "I was at Gymboree earlier, and I thought of you." Though he'd spoken several times of wanting to have children with me, this was the first time that I had, however vaguely, returned the sentiment.

He was quiet. "I talked to my mom," he said.

I didn't understand.

"She said that mental illness is genetic."

"Oh. Never mind, then," I said. "Forget I said anything. I didn't mean it."

At the time, I had been diagnosed for years with bipolar I disorder, formerly known as manic depression, and primarily characterized in the *DSM-IV*—the reference in use at the time—as a combination of alternating manic and depressive episodes. Symptoms of mania include a week or more of the following: grandiosity, such as believing one has magical powers; a severely decreased or nonexistent need for sleep; flights of ideas or racing thoughts; risky behaviors; impairment; and, in some cases, psychosis. Depression is characterized by two weeks or more of symptoms such as depressed mood, diminished interest or pleasure in nearly all activities, fatigue, and feelings of worthlessness. However, no textbook description of bipolar disorder can match the experience of the disorder itself. Kay Redfield Jamison writes, "There is a particular kind of pain, elation, loneliness, and terror involved in this kind of madness." I was diagnosed with bipolar disorder immediately prior to my freshman year at Yale University, twelve years before schizoaffective disorder made it onto the page.

At six o'clock I watched Stuart eat. He was on a restricted diet and seemed sullen about it. The other boys chatted about their first day, which had been fairly normal—there was some aggressive behavior, mild arguing, and a few mood swings here and there, though running around after the boys had not been as bad as I'd feared. In fact, I'd been quite cheerful looking at the wild turkeys with Julian while the others played soccer. But I worried about Stuart.

"How many gallons are in a liter?" he shouted in a robotic monotone.

The boys looked at him, confused.

"Point two-six-four! What's the largest dinosaur?"

Aaron snickered.

"Argentinosaurus!"

"Why are you asking us trivia questions?" Alex asked.

"They're not trivia questions," Stuart said stonily. "They're science facts."

Both Mark and Stuart had PDDs alongside their bipolar diagnoses. The most well-known PDD is autism; all PDDs involve delays in social interaction and communication. Mark had Asperger's, commonly referred to as a more high-functioning form of autism. Stuart had PDD-NOS, or PDD not otherwise specified. Mark, however, was far more high-functioning than Stuart, who seemed unable to carry on a conversation unless it involved shouting science facts or reciting, in savant-like detail, the plots of the Harry Potter movies. Aaron was the first to point this out.

"Stuart's a retard," he sang out as we bussed our dishes.

"Stop it," Stuart said, reddening.

"Isn't he a retard? Retard, retard. And a crybaby." Most of the temper tantrums that day had been Stuart's, usually due to a spat over game rules. He enjoyed playing games but exploded whenever a rule did not act in his favor.

The other boys, sensing that Aaron had become the alpha male, joined in the mockery. We counselors jumped in—"Hey, that's not cool"—but it wasn't enough, and even now I am not sure what I, as unprepared and unskilled as I was, should have done.

My younger brother and his wife had a child last year. I am now an aunt, and C. is an uncle. We met our niece on the day she was born, arriving at the luxurious hospital room to take photographs and coo over the newborn. I did not hold her; I still have not held her. She knows who I am and will smile and wave when she sees me, her nose crinkling up as her eyes narrow with pleasure. I love her more as time passes and she grows increasingly autonomous, becomes a person.

K.'s entrance into the world fills me with gut-churning anxiety. The world is in chaos. Earlier this year, a president whose platform rode on xenophobia and racism was inaugurated. I also fear that K. will, as my brother's daughter, inherit the genes that initiated me into the schizophrenias. I once read that to have a child is to be forever afraid, though that attitude may be applicable only to a certain type of parent; as K.'s aunt, I feel I must be vigilant when it comes to her mental health. Someday, if we are lucky, she will be a teenager. She will likely be feisty. At the same time, we know absolutely nothing about who she will end up becoming.

We counselors operated at Camp Wish—like most if not all parents— with little to no training and, though it pains me to say it, not much supervision. Because we were adults, the administrators at camp assumed that we'd act on our best instincts. If we came across a situation that we couldn't handle, they told us, we should contact someone higher up.

In the afternoon, after a fight at the pool table, C. took Stuart on a walk to cool down. Stuart told C. that he had no friends at camp. His mother had told him that he would be able to make friends at Camp Wish, where the other kids were just like him, but things at camp were the same as they were back home—and we had no idea what to do about it.

"I'm your friend," C. said.

"You're not a *kid* friend," Stuart replied.

That evening, when we were finally alone, C. said to me, "I just kept thinking about what school will be like for him when he starts middle school in the fall. He said he'd never had a friend in his life. It was just so goddamn sad."

One day I spotted a hummingbird near the low stone wall outside of the Camp Wish infirmary. When I pointed to it, Stuart shouted, "Hummingbirds flap their wings fifty times a second!"

Around eight o'clock in the morning each cabin traipsed to the infirmary. Campers were required to be on medication, and so everyone, from the nine-year-olds to the eighteen-year-olds, would line up and take their pills.

There was a wide variety of pills, kept in plastic bottles and baggies in tubs: mood stabilizers like Tegretol and Depakote and lithium; benzodiazepines for anxiety; antipsychotics; even antidepressants, which can potentially induce mania, etc. I had taken seven kinds of psychotropics in my lifetime and was taking four that summer. Because I didn't know if I was permitted to do so in front of the campers, I didn't take my medications at "meds time," opting instead to visit the infirmary later in the afternoon. I watched as a battalion of kids took their pills unblinkingly and without embarrassment, and then said good-bye to the nurses and reemerged into the fresh air. More unifying than camp songs, I thought.

"Retard," Alex muttered, and the boys pointed at Stuart, snickering.

C. had been speaking to Megan and the administrators regularly about Stuart since the teasing began; eventually the bullying became brutal enough for the administrators to decide that Stuart needed to be moved to the other preteen boys' cabin. C. and I gently informed Stuart, alone, that he was going to go to the next-door cabin, where things would hopefully be better for him. I was to be removed alongside Stuart and assigned to be his personal minder. Although Alex had bitten and kicked C., leaving a bruise that would last for weeks after camp, and Julian was suffering from constant hallucinations despite medication, Stuart needed the most care.

As C. and I prepared for the move, Stuart peered out the window and saw Aaron, Julian, Mark, and Alex playing touch football outside. "I want to play," he said. C. and I looked at each other apprehensively, but C. eventually took him outside, and I stood on the sidelines, where I watched Stuart quickly make a touchdown. I brimmed with gladness as he cheered and pranced about the field—even the other boys applauded his excellent footwork. But then one of them accidentally bumped into him in the middle of the game, which caused Stuart to scream. C. took him off the field as he hollered and flailed. The other boys yelled, "Crybaby! Crybaby!" after them.

C. and Stuart came into the cabin. "We're moving you now," C. said, trying to sound upbeat. He'd told me earlier that Megan and the head psychiatrist had recommended moving Stuart at a time when the other boys were distracted. "They won't notice that Stuart's gone, and probably won't say anything if they do," Megan had said. "They'll be too involved with their own business."

So I took Stuart and his bags to the other cabin. Stuart looked nervously in my direction—he couldn't make eye contact, a common symptom of PDD—and I sifted through the game box, looking for something for us to do with the least likelihood of causing a tantrum.

Then I heard the other boys come back to their cabin. "Hey, he's gone!" a voice cried. "The crybaby's gone!"

"Finally!"

"Woo!"

An eruption of yelling and cheering spilled from our former cabin. C. and the other counselors shouted for them to stop. Stuart's face twisted, and I hurried him away from the cabins, taking him to dinner. In our absence, Megan visited C.'s cabin and spoke to the boys about bullying. It turned out that all of them were bullied at their schools back home.

I read in the *New York Times* that a child of a parent who has bipolar disorder is thirteen times more likely to develop the disorder than a child of a parent who does not. A piece on *Salon* about madness and motherhood, written by a woman with bipolar disorder, evoked the following reader responses: "I grew up with a bipolar mother, and it made my childhood nightmarish"; "I know I'm supposed to say I'm glad I was born but [as a bipolar child of a bipolar mother, I] am not"; "Someone who is mentally unstable enough to require psychotropics should NOT, under any circumstances, even consider having a child." I read all sixty-eight comments. These I remember.

In back of the chorus of these internet commentators is my mother, who knew that she had a family history of mental illness when she became pregnant with me. At first, she was reticent about the breakdowns and suicides. As I grew older and my symptoms worsened, my mother at times expressed deep remorse and guilt at the fact that she had passed this "suffering" on to me, and presently tells me that I would be better off not having children. There are two issues here: one being the act of passing on a genetic burden, and the other being my ability, as a woman living with severe mental illness, to be a good mother.

At Yale and at Stanford, I commonly saw advertisements for egg donors in the backs of the *Yale Daily News*, the *Yale Herald*, and the *Stanford Daily*. The advertisements promised thousands of dollars for eggs from what was presumed to be good stock; I frequently met the SAT and GPA requirements, and occasionally met the ethnic requirements as well. To see me in the flesh and look over my curriculum vitae, one might be compelled to inquire after my eggs, which would eventually be rejected due to the advertisements' request for "healthy" donors.

Neither C. nor his mother was being cruel when they brought up their concern about my genetic and emotional fitness. That year was particularly bad. I became manic; went a week without sleeping more than two or three hours a night, or without sleeping at all; couldn't hold on to one thought without racing to another; scrawled ungrammatical nonsense in class; punched trees on Cross Campus. After the manias ran their course I became immobile, depressed, suicidal. I was hospitalized twice, for a total of twenty days. I had threatened to take an overdose once, had gone ahead and taken an overdose on a separate occasion, had been physically restrained in a bed in an ER, and had cut and burned myself innumerable times. C. and his mother were merely thinking about further consequences that I, surprisingly, had not thought of.

In the new cabin, life improved for Stuart. The new boys were far more patient with his social difficulties. Though he still had tantrums, and stalked off the field during another game of touch football, I do recall one thirty-minute session of Connect Four between Stuart and a particularly even-tempered camp veteran. I do not remember who won or lost.

Stuart was also quite funny. Upon being lowered from a ropes course that he refused to keep climbing, he joked with no embarrassment about feeling like "a ton of bricks on a construction site." He tended to conclude all jokes with a loud bark of a laugh: "*Ha!*"

C. covertly organized a get-together at the pool between Alex and Stuart, which I cosupervised. They played without incident for hours. "Look at how cute your fiancé is with those boys," another counselor said to me. "You must look forward to having children with him someday."

On the second, and final, night of camp, Stuart began to suffer from some sort of respiratory problem. The only complaints he had were that his spit was thick and that he "couldn't breathe right." "This always happens," he sobbed.

I took him to the infirmary. The doctor on call gave him his medication and inhaler and told him to go to bed early; I accompanied him to the empty cabin and he climbed into his top bunk, tears streaming.

"It feels so bad," he whispered.

"I know," I said. "Close your eyes."

I was barely tall enough to reach the top bunk standing on my tiptoes, but I stood as tall as I could so that I could see him. "It's okay," I whispered. He shuddered with discomfort, squeezing his eyes shut and periodically wiping tears away with the backs of his small hands. I told him to try and relax. I stroked his bangs with the palm of my hand. I hummed Chinese lullabies, and the longer I stood and stroked and hummed and whispered, the stiller he became, until he was asleep. At one point I saw, out of the corner of my eye, C.'s face in the window of the cabin.

Later he told me, "You would make a good mother."

"It was one night," I said.

The next morning, during closing ceremonies, the camp leaders instructed the campers to go around the circle and say something about their Camp Wish experience. The preteen cabins had experienced a chaotic breakfast—Aaron, who'd mocked Stuart for much of camp, curled up in a corner of the dining hall and refused to move, and one of the boys in Stuart's new cabin started screaming and crying about his need to go home, *immediately*.

In the circle, I sat in my folding chair and listened as each camper spoke about "making friends" and "belonging." Then it was Stuart's turn. He stood with his hands stuffed in his pockets. "At first, I didn't like camp," he said. "People were mean to me. And I didn't think I would make any friends. But then I had fun and I made some friends. And I want to come back next year."

I was glad then that I'd worn sunglasses, because I started to cry.

Would mental illness preclude me from being a good mother? I was fine at camp. I took care of the boys, and after I was removed from my first cabin, I took care of Stuart. But I hadn't been suffering from a mania or a depression then, and I can't imagine that I would have been allowed to care for someone else's children if I had. And since then, having developed psychotic symptoms that transformed my diagnosis into schizoaffective disorder, bipolar type, I've seen myself forget to feed my dog. I've seen myself remember, and then not care enough to do it. Sometimes I can't even say more than two words or move. There are periods when I know that my husband has been replaced by an identical robot.

My friend Amanda's mother has bipolar disorder. She was hospitalized one Christmas early in Amanda's life, and Amanda has hated Christmas ever since. My mentally ill great-aunt neglected her baby son so badly that she could no longer have custody of him. She died in a psychiatric hospital. One of my aunties tried to kill her husband with a chef's knife. Could I be one of these women?

Then again, mothers act badly all the time. Perhaps the bigger issue is that bad parenting is the problem, schizoaffective disorder or not. I might damage my future children in a way that has nothing to do with mania, depression, or psychosis. Or I might compensate for my neurological defects by being an especially good mother— one who reads stacks of parenting literature and educates her children early on about odd behavior that might come up at home.

Stuart's mother came to pick him up alone. She was a spry, cheerful woman who spoke to C. and me of Stuart's riding lessons. Due to some of her comments, C. and I later guessed that she was a single mother working to give Stuart the best life that he could have. When she left to gather Stuart's medications and paperwork from the infirmary, Stuart immediately entangled himself in an argument over air hockey.

"Let me play," he said to two girls who had just settled down at the table.

"We just got here," they said.

"Maybe you can watch them and then take a turn when they're done," I suggested.

"I want to play *now*," he said, voice rising.

And this would be the reality of being with Stuart, or any child with a difficulty. It would be for twenty-four hours a day, seven days a week, three hundred and sixty-five days a year. Not one day at camp, or three days, or three weeks. A lifetime. Stuart's mother eventually returned with his things, hugged him, and told him that it was time to go.

Stuart did not say good-bye to either C. or me. He just left, and we haven't seen him since.

On the drive home C. and I were, at first, quiet.

"We could have a child like that," I finally said.

A cousin to my mother's remorse and guilt is an invisible, additional question that I have for her, that being: would it have been better if I'd never been born? Even though I've made my parents proud, I can't help but wonder if that outweighs watching me break down over the years. Perhaps if my mother had been able to choose my genetics, she would've rearranged some things. I would be someone else entirely.

For all my fears about constantly watching over a child with mental illness, or any other severe disability, the very reasons that I thought I didn't want children might be the ultimate factors that would end up changing my mind. I was surprised by my love for Stuart. He was smart and hilarious, and knew a lot of fascinating trivia. He and I also shared a diagnosis, and perhaps that, most of all, is why I had patience for his tantrums and oddities. "We could have a child like that," I'd said—and indeed, we could.

After I had my IUD removed for medical reasons, C. and I began to discuss more-permanent forms of contraception. We talk about tubal ligation, Essure, and a vasectomy. And yet I insist that I don't want a tubal ligation or Essure. I tell C. that a vasectomy would have more of a possibility of reversal. When I ask myself why I care about a possible reversal, I realize that I don't know.

I had abdominal surgery in my late twenties. There was a giant cyst on my left ovary, and it needed to be removed; it had been possible that I would lose my ovary along with the cyst. When I woke up, the first thing that I remember asking the nurse was, "Is my ovary okay?"

She nodded. "Your ovary is fine," she said. And then she added, "You already asked. When you came out of the general anesthesia, those were the first words out of your mouth."

On the Ward

With Level One privileges at the psychiatric hospital where I was involuntarily committed in 2002, the patient was allowed off the ward for breakfast. Because I spent my first half day hidden in my room's wardrobe, sobbing, no one knew that I was not a danger to myself or others, and so I ate the first breakfast without any designation, stowed away near the nurses' station at a round plastic table. I chose raisin bran from a selection of preschool-sized boxes. I ate the cereal under supervision with a plastic spoon. I drank apple juice, which came in a plastic container with a foil top and a straw. There were patients who had been there longer, were well behaved, and yet also ate breakfast on the ward; signs hung on the doors of their rooms indicated that they received electroconvulsive therapy, and thus could not eat before their morning treatments.

The nurse who checked my vitals on the second morning informed me that I'd been elevated to Level One status, which I took as a good sign. I sat by the television for a while with some of the other patients, all of whom were groggy from psychotropic side effects and uncommunicative.

Eventually Level One patients began to hang around the ward exit, as though it were a gate at an airport terminal, and we were all eager to nab overhead bin space. A handful of nurses followed, laughing among themselves and teasing: "You say that to me again, I dare you." "Yeah, I'll say that to you again." One nurse used her key card to scan us out of the ward—the double doors swung slowly open—and we went down in pairs in the elevator, which required another key card, to the cafeteria. The room was a smaller version of the school cafeterias I've known all my life, with a line for hot food and a few circular tables. The other patients muttered and jostled, jittery in this foreign space.

We did not serve ourselves. Instead, we told the servers what we wanted. I asked for eggs and home fries, and could tell straightaway that the scoop of yellow dropped on my plate was reconstituted. My stomach lurched at the sight, but I was hungry, having barely eaten in weeks.

Where to sit? I had a sense of which patients to avoid and which would let me be, but I also saw a few sitting with the nurses, who attracted me with their normalcy. I took a risk and sat at an empty table, where I attended to the food before me. I used my spork first to sample the eggs, which were nearly tasteless, and lacked the near-sulfurous attributes that make them disgusting to those who hate eggs—but their tastelessness was its own challenge. I almost choked on the first bite before abandoning the rest. The home fries were warm and slicked my tongue with grease. I ate them all. I finished my plastic container of apple juice and looked around: the glass door and windows showed the bright blue sky we couldn't reach; the nurses ate and chatted as if we could be anywhere.

An "asylum" is a "place of haven or safety" (*The Oxford English Dictionary*), though the antiquated word, when applied to psychiatric hospitals, is now used to conjure fear. In the book *Haunted Asylums: Stories of the Damned; Inside the Haunted Prisons, Wards, and Crazy Houses*, paranormal enthusiast Roger P. Mills claims that mental hospitals "are among the most haunted places on the planet." The second season of the FX horror series *American Horror Story*, called "Asylum," places a mishmash of murderers, a secret Nazi, rape, and grotesque scientific experiments within the walls of its fictional sanitarium, Briarcliff Manor. The Elizabeth Arkham Asylum for the Criminally Insane confines, at least temporarily, the worst villains of *Batman* lore. The word "asylum" triggers cultural associations, à la *One Flew Over the Cuckoo's Nest*, with frightening and brutal treatment of psychiatric patients. And yet I suspect that what's truly scary about the word has more to do with the inefficacy of psychiatric treatment from that era, which did little to rein in its patients' most disturbing behaviors, including those that were inexplicable, dangerous, or violent.

"[The patients] were being driven to a prison, through no fault of their own, in all probability for life. In comparison, how much easier it would be to walk to the gallows than to this tomb of living humans!" writes investigative journalist Nellie Bly in her 1887 exposé, *Ten Days in a Mad-House*, which gives readers a revelatory view into a New York City "lunatic asylum." Bly gained access to the hospital by pretending to be insane herself.

After her admittance, Bly recounts asking for her notebook and pencil. The attending nurse, Miss Grady, tells her that she brought only a book, and no pencil. "I was provoked," Bly says, "and insisted that I had, whereupon I was advised to fight against the imaginations of my brain."

In another part of *Ten Days*, she says, "I always made a point of telling the doctors I was sane and asking to be released, but the more I endeavored to assure them of my sanity the more they doubted it."

During my second hospitalization, which occurred in the same location as my first, I passed a nurse.

"How are you doing?" she asked.

"Okay," I said, which was true. My mania and subsequent depression seemed to have been exorcised by the overdose I'd taken immediately prior to being hospitalized, and other than being frustrated by my return to the WS2 ward, life no longer felt like an intolerable sentence.

The nurse smiled. "But how are you *really* doing?"

"I'm *really* doing okay."

The notes I've acquired from Yale Psychiatric Institute read, among other things, "Patient shows lack of insight."

As Bly's anecdotes, and my own, indicate, a primary feature of the experience of staying in a psychiatric hospital is that you will not be believed about anything. A corollary to this feature: things will be believed about you that are not at all true.

My third hospitalization occurred in rural Louisiana. I told the doctor that I was a writer and had studied psychology at Yale and Stanford, which was about as believable as my saying that I was an astronaut and an identical twin born to a Russian ambassador. I later trounced the other patients in a mandatory group therapy word game, not allowing anyone else to score a point; to do so was childish, but I was tired of being treated as though I were stupid. I do not know how my behavior in this session reflected on me from the nurses' and doctor's perspectives. It may have indicated that I was intelligent, or at least book-smart, two characteristics that are of dubious value in a psychiatric hospital. It almost certainly indicated that I can be a stubborn asshole.

The doctor told me in one of our rare meetings that I'd said, upon emergency room intake, that I believed in "a conspiracy of people" who were determined to hurt me.

"I didn't say that," I said. "I said that I was feeling *unsafe*." But "feeling unsafe"—as in, feeling terror about everything and nothing in particular—was an unfortunate phrase for me to use during the intake. "Unsafe" is a psychiatric code word for "suicidal," which I was not, although I was many other things. I hadn't said anything about a conspiracy. "Unsafe" might have triggered the hospital's belief—its own delusion—that I felt unsafe due to a paranoid belief: a conspiracy of people out to do me harm.

The hospital maintained for the remainder of my stay that I had come in feeling "unsafe," with delusions of persecution. Because "unsafe" doubled as "suicidal," I was considered a danger to myself. Even though I had voluntarily walked into the ER for help, "unsafe" meant that I was considered to be "involuntarily hospitalized," which also meant that I was locked down in the rural Louisiana hospital, on the north shore of Lake Pontchartrain, until the doctor gave me permission to leave. I did not know how long that would be.

Things had gone wrong prior to that stay during the time I spent alone in the Metairie hotel room.

I'd had problems with hotel rooms that year. Once, C. took me with him to Reno on a business trip and left me in our room while he attended a conference. In his absence, a wild fear came over me. I covered the mirrors with towels; when that wasn't enough to soothe me, I hid in the tiny closet. C. came back. He saw the towels on the mirrors, and he began to call my name. Eventually he tried to open the closet door, where I was still hiding, and I emitted a small scream.

"Don't open the door," I whimpered.

Recounting this anecdote without providing a porthole to my inner workings makes it sound like a prototypical tale of a lunatic, and I don't dispute that I was insane in Reno. I did, however, possess insight into my own situation. I'd brought my laptop into the closet with me, and was coherently messaging a friend about how I'd wound up there. I'd covered the mirrors because the sight of my own face terrified me. No story accompanied the fear—no hallucinations about torn and rotting flesh, no delusions about losing my soul to the reflection. As was the case months later in Louisiana, I was overwhelmed with a sense of free-floating terror that spread like blood and congealed around vulnerable targets such as my face, the patterns in the carpet and on the bedspread, the view of dry and dusty Reno from our window. The only tenable solution was to fold myself into a small, dark place: the closet. Typing on my laptop, I tried to explain to my friend what was happening. Perhaps I was attempting to provide evidence for my side of the story, or trying to make sense of a situation that was confusing even to me, using tools that I found acceptable. The small chat window was not frightening in the same way that a face-to-face interaction would have been.

C. just came back, I typed. *I'm scared.*

Eventually, I emerged. I was calmer, but fragile. The smallest pressure would crush me. We had no warnings of what those pressures were.

When we returned to San Francisco, I went back to work. From 10 a.m. to 6 p.m., Monday through Friday, I went to stand-up meetings and gave presentations and sat at my computer and covertly swigged from the liquor in the office pantry. I did my job. I said nothing about the horror show that was still sinking its teeth into me. Sometimes I saw things darting here and there, but I ignored them. I considered myself lucky to have hallucinations that I could ignore.

My psychotic symptoms were barely under control, but C. and I had an upcoming trip to his parents' home in New Orleans. We discussed canceling and staying in San Francisco. We wondered if being around family during the holidays would, instead of providing more stress, actually be the best thing for both of us. After all, C. had been my primary caretaker during this long crisis, and I suspected that spreading the responsibility among a stable group, particularly one that was loving, would ease the strain.

So we flew south, watching the olive-hued swampland grow in the airplane's window, and stayed in a motel near his parents' suburban home. We fell with relief into the arms of our welcoming family.

On one of those nights, when the air was damp and cold, C. left to watch a football game at the Superdome with his father, and I was once again alone in an unfamiliar room. I'd encouraged him to go—I was glad that he had the opportunity to do something fun without me. But his absence undid something that needed to be fastened shut, and the terror was glad to sweep in. I started gathering towels. The coherence of reality threatened to desert me. Soon my mind was a black hole, and that dead star insisted on snatching every wisp and scrap of sense; it tore at the edges of the world. After struggling with the decision to reach out, I called my mother-in-law. I told her as calmly as I could that I thought I might need to be in a hospital.

"All right," she said. A former hospital nurse, Ms. Gail has a soothing demeanor in times of crisis. "Let's go ahead and get you sorted."

Though nearly all the statements a psychiatric patient can make are not believed, proclamations of insanity are the exception to the rule.

"I want to kill myself" generally holds water, and a therapist who hears those words is legally required to disclose them to prevent client self-harm. In a study hypothesizing that sane people could easily be hospitalized under certain conditions, researcher David Rosenhan and his associates claimed to have auditory hallucinations, and were consequently held in different psychiatric facilities for an average of nineteen days—this, despite being neurotypical and exhibiting no symptoms while hospitalized. All but one of the pseudopatients were released with diagnoses of schizophrenia, and were released only on the condition that they agree to take antipsychotic prescriptions. If not for Rosenhan's credibility as a scientist and the ensuing publication of his 1973 paper "On Being Sane in Insane Places," those diagnoses could have dogged Rosenhan and his compatriots for life. Unlike me, Rosenhan ultimately proved to the doctors he had duped that he was, really and truly, a Stanford researcher.

In the Louisiana hospital I stood in a slow cafeteria line. While waiting to reach the workers who would deliver the morning's hot and greasy victuals, I realized that Mara, my roommate, who stood in front of me, was wearing my coat—a well-made, beloved tweed garment that I'd owned for years.

I asked, "Are you wearing my coat?"

She didn't respond at first. I'd noticed that Mara had the slowed-down disposition of someone who was either locked in a severe depression or burned-out on psychotropics. She turned her head, not making eye contact, and began to take off my coat in slow motion.

"It's okay," I assured her. "You can keep it on during breakfast, but I'd like it back when we go upstairs."

Despite this, she finished removing my coat and handed it to me without saying a word.

The next morning, I awoke to something unexpected: a nurse in our room, dropped to a crouch by my roommate's bed. She said, gently, "I see you have three pillows there. Do you have an extra pillow, Mara?"

I sat up, turned, and saw the single pillow on my bed. Mara had taken one of my pillows while I was asleep.

I said, "I'm missing one of mine."

When the nurse brought me back the pillow Mara had pilfered during the night, I mentioned the incident with my coat as well. I wasn't trying to get Mara in trouble—the thefts were so bizarre, and Mara so absent of malice, that it seemed impossible she would be punished for them—but I did want someone in authority to know that they were happening.

The nurse replied, her voice low, "Mara doesn't mean to do it. She can't help it. But I would recommend that you keep anything important or valuable with the nurses' desk."

There was one important thing that I would have been devastated to have anyone take: my green notebook with a textured cover like alligator skin. I'd been able to keep it at all times because it was perfect-bound, with no spiral wire that I could use to harm myself or others. I was so wedded to my notebook that one of the other patients was convinced that I was an undercover journalist, and nicknamed me Lois Lane; Lois Lane, and not Nellie Bly, whose asylum exposé instigated an $850,000 increase in the budget of the New York City Department of Public Charities and Correction. I never learned the diagnosis of the young man who called me Lois, and he claimed that he had no idea why he was in the hospital. I couldn't tell if there was anything wrong with him.

In *Ten Days*, Bly writes: "The insane asylum on Blackwell's Island is a human rat-trap. It is easy to get in, but once there it is impossible to get out."

Both David Rosenhan and Nellie Bly knew during their institutionalizations that they would never be caught in their rat-traps beyond what they could endure. Having been hospitalized through trickery, they would only have to reveal those trickeries to escape. I doubt they ever felt the absolute terror that coincides with not knowing when, or if, you will get out of such a place.

In a psychiatric hospital, getting out is known as "discharge," which is a sacred word. Rumors circulate among the patients about who will be discharged soon and when; morning group therapy sessions note and celebrate whoever will be discharged that day; rare visits from psychiatrists, or, in some cases, a single psychiatrist for the entire ward, revolve around the patient's potential discharge date. Though discharge might not be on the table for several days, the question of when it will happen hovers over everything as soon as a patient walks in.

The obsession with discharge is most prominent among those who are involuntarily hospitalized, as I have been, because those who've checked themselves in are permitted to leave at any time. I've watched people who seemed no more or less sane than I did decide, perhaps, that they'd had enough of being watched over and told what to do and think, where and when to sleep, or simply that they were feeling better, and those people checked themselves out as easily as leaving a hotel while the rest of us continued to count the interminable hours, the interminable days.

In the winter of 2003, because I had technically taken an overdose of anticonvulsants—although such a minor overdose that there was no need for charcoal, or for pumping my stomach—I was put in two-point restraints while waiting in the ER for an ambulance. The restraints were leather, and kept one wrist and one ankle shackled to the bed while I lay and listened to the calls of people in pain, and the response of the harried people trying to help them.

At one point during the hours of waiting, I grew bored and tried to wriggle my hand out of its cuff. It worked because I have fine-boned hands with delicate, strong wrists—piano hands. When a nurse realized I'd turned my two-point restraints into a one-point restraint, he tightly fastened my hand back into the cuff. Before he walked away, he threatened to put me in four-point restraints if I didn't behave.

For schizophrenia, second-generation antipsychotics are considered the first line of attack (or defense, depending on your perspective), and include Abilify, Saphris, Rexulti, Vraylar, Clorazil, Fanapt, Latuda, Zyprexa, Invega, Seroquel, Risperdal, and Geodon. Less preferable are the first-generation antipsychotics—chlorpromazine, fluphenazine, haloperidol, and perphenazine—which are infamous for their neurological side effects. Most notably, first-generation antipsychotics can cause involuntary jerking motions of the face and limbs, known as tardive dyskinesia (TD); once activated, TD may remain as a side effect even after you quit taking the medication that caused it.

A person who is hospitalized with schizophrenia will inevitably be put on some type of second-generation antipsychotic. Zyprexa, for example, is known to put the brakes on manic activity. Hospitalization is generally reserved for times of psychiatric crisis, and so Zyprexa, or a drug like it, may shut down the most violent behaviors.

But medication is only one part of the ideal treatment plan. According to the American Psychiatric Association's *Practice Guideline for the Treatment of Patients with Schizophrenia*, second edition, that plan has three major components: "1) [to] reduce or eliminate symptoms, 2) [to] maximize quality of life and adaptive functioning, and 3) [to] promote and maintain recovery from the debilitating effects of illness to the maximum extent possible." All of this should be done swiftly; according to a 2012 study, the average stay in a psychiatric hospital is ten days—the exact length of time I was institutionalized during each of my three hospital visits. The contemporary psychiatric hospital is intended to stabilize its patients, and then to set them up for recovery in the outside world.

State mental hospitals—the type referred to as asylums, and of which Nellie Bly wrote in her landmark book—were long seen as terrible, frightening places that were nevertheless essential for a society with mentally ill and developmentally disabled people in it. Despite this, the publication of Albert Q. Maisel's exposé "Bedlam 1946: Most U.S. Mental Hospitals Are a Shame and a Disgrace," in *Life* magazine, awoke Americans to the gruesome nature of such asylums as nothing had before, breathlessly announcing that "state after state has allowed its institutions for the care and the cure of the mentally sick to degenerate into little more than concentration camps on the Belsen pattern." Advocates such as Dr. Robert H. Felix, who became the first director of the National Institute of Mental Health in the 1950s, followed suit; Felix believed that state mental hospitals could and should be replaced by federally funded community health centers, which were not only believed to be more humane, but which also paved the way for the recovery model of mental health treatment.

The decision to do away with state mental hospitals remains a controversial one, and is blamed by some for everything from homelessness to murder. In his book *American Psychosis: How the Federal Government Destroyed the Mental Illness Treatment System*, E. Fuller

Torrey rails against the nationwide closing of state mental hospitals that occurred under President John F. Kennedy:

> Unfortunately, the mental health centers legislation passed by Congress was fatally flawed. It encouraged the closing of state mental hospitals without any realistic plan regarding what would happen to the discharged patients, especially those who refused to take the medication they needed to remain well. It included no plan for the future funding of the [community] mental health centers. It focused resources on prevention when nobody understood enough about mental illnesses to know how to prevent them. And by bypassing the states, it guaranteed that future services would not be coordinated.

Torrey, a psychiatrist who helped found the Treatment Advocacy Center, is a vigorous proponent of involuntary treatment, including hospitalization. He has publicly criticized the recovery movement for giving false hope to the severely ill; in turn, recovery and survivor-based movements criticize Torrey for his emphasis on drugging them and locking them up.

There are solid reasons behind the existence of involuntary hospitalization laws—primarily, that there are circumstances in which persons with severe mental illness become unable to make good choices for themselves. The National Alliance on Mental Illness (NAMI) states in its policy platform that "with adequate professional consultation, every person with a serious mental illness who has the capacity and competence to do so should be entitled to manage his or her own treatment," but that "when an individual lacks capacity and competence because of his or her serious mental illness . . . the substitute judgment of others . . . may be justified in determining treatment and possible hospitalization." Regarding involuntary commitment, NAMI makes a point of mentioning that people "with serious mental illnesses such as schizophrenia and bipolar disorder" may "at times, due to their illness, lack insight or good judgment about their need for medical treatment." As a woman with schizoaffective disorder, the psychiatric disorder that combines the two, I consider myself called. Involuntary commitment may sometimes be warranted, but it has never felt useful to me.

Section 5150 of the California Welfare and Institutions Code states that "a person, as a result of a mental health disorder, [who] is a danger to others, or to himself or herself, or gravely disabled" is allowed to be taken "into custody for a period of up to 72 hours for assessment, evaluation, and crisis intervention, or placement for evaluation and treatment in a facility designated by the county for evaluation and treatment and approved by the State Department of Health Care Services." Although all states have some form of this law, "5150" has slipped into the cultural vernacular as a catchall term for involuntary psychiatric hospitalization. A friend of mine, a veteran of the mental health care system, once confessed to me that his ATM card's PIN code was 5150. We both laughed, uneasily.

According to section (g)(1) of Section 5150, a person taken under custody due to the law must be provided the following information, either orally or in writing:

My name is———.
I am a [peace officer/mental health professional] with [name of agency].

You are not under criminal arrest, but I am taking you for an examination by mental health professionals at [name of facility].

You will be told your rights by the mental health staff.

If the person is taken under custody while at home, the following must also be provided:

> You may bring a few personal items with you, which I will have to approve. Please inform me if you need assistance turning off any appliance or water. You may make a phone call and leave a note to tell your friends or family where you have been taken.

Though I've lived in California for most of my life, I've never been 5150'd. I do find that this final paragraph echoes the wording of kidnapping narratives—"leave a note to tell your friends or family where you have been taken." What do these notes, written under duress, look like? How much time is a person given in order to concoct such a message?

I once interviewed a young woman, whom I will call Kate, about her 5150 experience. Kate tells me that she was 5150'd in 2012, after confessing suicidal ideation to a social worker at a welfare office in Oakland, California. She was facing eviction, and, she admits, was not handling it well. The social worker offered to have Kate speak to the counselor on duty; Kate agreed, relieved to be offered help. However, once it became clear that the counselor wasn't on duty, the social worker had Kate 5150'd instead. Kate doesn't remember hearing anything like the Section 5150 (g)(1) script, though she also recalls that nobody, including the police, said much until she got to the hospital.

"I don't know how anyone gets better in [that place]," she says. "They put me in the big crazy intake room. Most people seemed to be homeless people that needed a few days off the street to catch up on sleep and get some proper meals. Some people were the rambling or screaming type. Some seemed to be regulars. There was no care. I just sat there with the nurses and begged them to let me go." Her experience influenced the way she responds to other people in psychiatric crisis. "Now," she says, "I do everything I can to keep people from being involuntarily taken and offer to drive them to the ER myself. . . . I'm a nobody and I know how to calm someone down long enough to get them to consent [to hospitalization voluntarily]."

Though the experience of being 5150'd is not the same as being arrested ("You are not under criminal arrest"), there are inevitable parallels between involuntary hospitalization and incarceration. In both circumstances, a confined person's ability to control their life and their body is dramatically reduced; they are at the mercy of those in control; they must behave in prescribed ways to acquire privileges and eventually, perhaps, to be released. And then there is the wide swath of people for whom mental illness and imprisonment overlap: according to the Department of Justice, "nearly 1.3 million people with mental illness are incarcerated in state and federal jails and prisons."

For those of us living with severe mental illness, the world is full of cages where we can be locked in.

My hope is that I'll stay out of those cages for the rest of my life, although I allow myself the option of checking into a psychiatric ward if suicide feels like the only other option. I maintain, years later, that not one of my three involuntary hospitalizations helped me. I believe that being held in a psychiatric ward against my will remains among the most scarring of my traumas.

I am no longer friends with the man who told me his pin code was 5150, but when we were kin I spent countless hours trying to convince him not to kill himself. On the dark nights when it seemed particularly likely that he would end his life, I'd attempt to coax him into voluntary hospitalization; if he were in a hospital, so I reasoned, I'd know that someone was keeping an eye on him. Once, during a particularly bad spell, I told him that I was going to call the police. He laughed and said he'd get the cops to shoot him before he'd let them take him to yet another psychiatric facility. He was tired of hospitals, and he was tired of living, but I never had to ask him why he was so resistant to the idea of hospitalization. I think we both knew that I, too, feared being on a ward again.

The Slender Man,
the Nothing, and Me

Bespectacled, blond Morgan Geyser in an interrogation room says casually of Payton "Bella" Leutner, "She's the one who was stabbed. Is she dead? I was just wondering." Her words were caught on camera in *Beware the Slenderman*, an HBO documentary about the mythos of "the Slender Man" and its role in two twelve-year-olds' stabbing of a third girl. The Slender Man, according to lore, kidnaps and preys on children, and is purported to have been in existence for centuries. "Go ballistic" is the instruction that Anissa Weier is said to have given to Morgan, her partner-in-crime, who stabbed Payton nineteen times in the woods. When asked by the man who found Payton crawling out of the woods, "Who did this to you?" Payton Leutner responds, "My best friend."

I began to be truly afraid when the camera moves to Morgan's father, Matt, a man with schizophrenia who has, at that moment, only recently learned of his daughter's diagnosis with the same disorder. He is stricken and tearful as he says, "I wish I could talk to her about . . . I always wanted to know, like, if she sees that stuff too." He says, "I know the devil's not in the backseat, but the devil is in the backseat."

In the case of the Slender Man, the "devil in the backseat" originated on the Creepypasta Wiki, an online series of documents and forums full of grim, fantastical tales told with utter conviction. Wikis are designed to grow; essentially anyone may contribute to a wiki, something crucial to remember when considering the attributions of urban legends under the guise of horror stories. According to the wiki, the faceless Slender Man wears a suit and has long, slender arms and legs. Tentacles protrude from his back. He wears a hat, although the type of hat varies depending on the source. He kidnaps children in particular, and preys on them upon capture. The wiki includes historical references ranging from Brazilian cave paintings to Egyptian hieroglyphics to German woodcuts. The Slender Man, according to the wiki, is tied to legends from around the world (Scottish, Dutch, and German myths are cited). In one well-known Slender Man document, a sullen girl stands in the foreground of a black-and-white photograph amid a group of children who look like campers. The image is low-res, like a photo from an 1980s yearbook. A tall, skinny white figure stands in the background—it could be a sculpture, but is, of course, the Slender Man. The caption reads: "1986, photographer Mary Thomas, went missing in 1986."

Says one user in the forums, "This is probably one of the most classic creppypasta [sic]. Unfournely [sic] its [sic] been so chlichaed [sic] that its [sic] getting old, just like Jeff the killer. However its [sic] still a classic." In response, another user says, "anyone remember that news article where a young girl killed her friend(s) to 'appease' slenderman?? yeeah." A third user chimes in, "I remember that. I miss the good ol' days." Folklorist Trevor J. Blank says in *Beware the Slenderman*, "Often in the adult world we forget how much it sucks to be a kid."

In scrambling to find an explanation for Payton's attempted murder, investigators looked to other cases of youth violence: were Anissa and Morgan bullied, as in the case of the Columbine shooters? Bullying did not seem to be a major issue. The girls had each other, and they had Payton—in fact, the stabbing occurred on the day after a sleepover birthday party for Morgan. I posit that being a kid "sucks" even without the specters of bullying or abuse. You have no control over your life; it is frequently impossible to decode the actions of adults. The internet is one way to access a type of freedom. Because of my father's job as a computer engineer, I was using the internet before the World Wide Web was made available to the public, and learned to "make friends" on Prodigy bulletin boards when none of my peers were aware of such things—the drama, the flirting, the expensive long-distance calls with "internet people"— and I am fascinated by the role of the internet in Anissa's life in particular. The browser history on Anissa's iPad revealed a whirlwind of searches, including "The Sanity Test," "The Psychopath Test," and "The Sociopath Test." She was accessing ways of exploring the world and her place in it. Another video she watched included a snake eating a mouse. Says her mother, "She liked to spend a lot of private time up in her room . . . I totally regret the iPad." And, of course, the internet is where Anissa learned of the Slender Man.

Many online documents testify to the Slender Man's existence. One is a so-called police report from 1993, with "blood" spattered on the document. Childish handwriting says atop the typing, "SLENDER MAN KILL US ALREADY KILL US KILL KILL KILL." Another is a poorly Photoshopped newspaper clipping with the headline "Local Boy Disappears." "School officials state that in the weeks leading up to his disappearance, that he had been irritable at school and home, after complaining of a tall, very thin man in all black. Police declined to comment at this time." At the bottom are the words: "**Alert**Alert**Deployment request**Anti-S Walker Unit to deploy to —— Wichita —— Kansas." These "primary documents," however badly cobbled together, are presented as genuine and accurate artifacts; they are PDFs and images created by people excited to coax the Slender Man story into life, and the more realistic, the better.

"I told [Morgan] about [the Slender Man]," Anissa testified.

"Anissa told me we had to," Morgan said. "[Anissa] said that he'd kill our families."

Anissa might have been the one to discover Slender Man, but there exist pages and pages of Morgan's disturbing drawings of him. She claims that she saw the Slender Man when she was five years old, long before she saw any internet artifacts about the monster. But the audience for such artifacts is made up of people—or children—like Anissa Weier and Morgan Geyser, whose dual obsession with the Slender Man led to a conspiracy to kill their mutual friend Payton Leutner. The three girls would go to Skateland to celebrate Morgan's birthday, after which there would be a sleepover in Morgan's basement. Originally, the plan was to kill Payton and hide her under the covers. The murder would turn Anissa and Morgan into Slender Man's "proxies," and they would live with Slender Man in his mansion forever.

Payton Leutner did not die after the stabbing, though people seem to think she was killed—when I mentioned working on this essay, friends and acquaintances recounted a murder, though what actually happened was this: On May 31, 2014, in Waukesha, Wisconsin, twelve-year-olds Anissa Weier and Morgan Geyser conspired to kill Payton "Bella" Leutner, who was then considered to be Morgan's best friend. On the morning after a birthday sleepover, the girls went to a playground and then a public restroom, where the stabbing did not happen. In the nearby woods, Anissa ultimately told Morgan to kill Payton with a knife they'd brought with them, saying, "Go ballistic." Morgan stabbed Payton nineteen times. ("I don't like screaming," Anissa later said.) A passerby discovered Payton crawling out of the woods and called 911. Police ultimately found Anissa and Morgan walking along the interstate.

For me, a popular 1984 film called *The NeverEnding Story* stood in place of the Slender Man's well-wrought wiki. I was in second grade when the film was released. An expensive West German production full of fantastic creatures, the film follows Bastian, a bookish and bullied boy, and his absorption into an alternate universe called Fantasia, which happens via a mysterious book snatched from a dusty bookstore. In Fantasia, the mystical Childlike Empress has fallen ill, and a young hero, Atreyu, is sent on a quest to find a cure. Meanwhile, a terrible force called the Nothing is destroying their world. If the Childlike Empress survives, it is thought, so will Fantasia. By the end of the film, Bastian's and Atreyu's worlds intersect. It is up to Bastian to save Fantasia by giving the Childlike Empress a new name, which he does by screaming out of a window during a violent storm.

I was the leader when it came to bringing Fantasia and the Nothing into our lives, tempted by the idea that we might be part of a larger story without fully knowing how. I told my best friend, Jessica, that we were part of a book, and that the book was being written as we acted. Jessica had frizzy hair that was difficult to tame, and she was prone to tears, a trait that I found exhausting.

We coaxed a third friend, Katie, into the game, which grew increasingly elaborate—if we said the word "Nothing," or if we stepped into the sunlight from shadow, we would become hypnotized and walk around like zombies. We referred constantly to the bigger world in which someone was reading a book about us and what we were doing, gesturing skyward to indicate that we were merely fictions in someone else's story. This went on until Katie finally insisted that we were only playing. No, Jessica and I insisted, we were not playing. It was real, all of it. We stuck to our story until Katie cried and ran from us; at this point, Jessica and I had an unspoken understanding that the Nothing was an important part of our lives, and we would not toss it aside for anything. The next day, Katie returned to say that she'd spoken to her parents about us and our game. Her parents, she said, had reassured her that Jessica and I were indeed only playing.

But this did not stop us. Jessica and I kept zoning out when we stepped into the light. We were careful not to say the Nothing's name.

The game continued until a critical conflict occurred between Jessica and me, not long after Katie's insistence that we were lying and her subsequent departure from our group of friends. Cautiously, secretively, Jessica approached me.

"We're just playing, aren't we?" she asked, hushed.

"We're not playing," I replied. "This is real."

"No, really," she said.

I repeated, "*We're not playing.*"

Jessica insisted that I tell her the truth. With my every denial, she became increasingly hysterical while I remained calm. I watched her leave in sobs; I remained grounded in the world of my imagination.

Imagination has a power in childhood that it lacks in older years. How much more rooted in my childhood delusions would I have been had I—like Anissa and Morgan—had access to scores of documents that testified to the reality of my daydreams? What if I'd been able to open YouTube and watch other children being swept away by the power of the Nothing? Would I have become increasingly absorbed by the narrative, and stuck to the story to dangerous ends, if I had spent hours reading hundreds of forum posts about its veracity?

Though I wasn't diagnosed with schizoaffective disorder till much later, I am intrigued by my second-grade willingness to forgo even friendship for the sake of my version of unreality. Was there already something vulnerable to fragility lurking deep in my mind, or was I simply more stubborn than most? In hindsight, I ask myself how much I truly believed in my own fiction. Where the puzzle gets tricky is in children's natural proclivity for the line between *fake* and *real*. Even now, C. and I treat our childhood stuffed animals with a tenderness that indicates that we believe, to some degree, that they are sentient. Yet if a fellow adult asked us whether we actually think they are thinking creatures, as Real as the Velveteen Rabbit, we would have to say no. (And then feel guilty, deep down, about betraying our stuffed pals.)

I eventually became friends with Jessica again, sacrificing my adherence to our version of Fantasia in order to repair our relationship. To do so sounds simple, but I don't think it was so simple for me to detach from the world we'd created, as though I could simply toss it aside after a period of intense commitment. When I try to remember how I gave up the fiction, my mind blots out the transition; I have no recollection of telling Jessica that there was no Nothing and no Fantasia, as though the trauma of letting it all go had shattered my memories.

I postponed watching *Beware the Slenderman* for weeks after I knew I'd be writing this essay. I insisted on watching the documentary with C., who would serve as an anchor to reality, and I insisted that we watch it during the day, for fear that my adult self would become seduced and haunted by the idea of the Slender Man. I ended up viewing the film while visiting my friend Miriam. We watched it on my laptop, reclining on her sofa bed, while Brooklyn and Manhattan loomed outside her apartment windows. I tried to hold myself at a distance by taking notes in a small green notebook as we watched the terrible story unravel.

According to a testifying psychiatrist in the film, Dr. Kenneth Casimir, "Schizophrenia is one of the most serious and one of the most studied mental illnesses of human beings." He also says, "It bears saying that schizophrenia, in and of itself, is not a dangerous illness. There are many thirty-five-year-olds who have schizophrenia who don't have to be incarcerated, who can be managed in a community. However, there's a second part to that. When your delusion—when your fixed delusion tells you to kill people, and when your insight doesn't allow you to seek treatment, then schizophrenia becomes dangerous." I was thirty-four when Miriam and I watched this. It can be said that I am "managed in a community." I do not consider myself to be dangerous.

The final trials concerning Anissa Weier and Morgan Geyser occurred in September and October 2017, in their hometown of Waukesha, Wisconsin. Both were charged as adults, with attempted first-degree murder in Morgan's case and attempted second-degree murder in Anissa's case; both used the insanity defense. A mental disorder defense indicates that a person falls in one of two categories: that they were acting from "the irresistible impulse," in which they could not stop themselves; or that their mental disorder prevented them from realizing that what they were doing was wrong.

DA Kevin Osborne said of the girls, "They knew this was wrong. They understood what they were doing was wrong."

Osborne said that Anissa may have believed that the Slender Man was real, but that she had the mental capacity to know that she was committing a crime. Anissa Weier was diagnosed with a "shared delusional disorder," or schizotypy, a milder form of schizophrenia. One characteristic of schizotypy is magical ideation, which would seem to provide a fertile ground for fully believing in the Slender Man.

Though it has been posited that Anissa was the ringleader of the attack on Payton, it was Morgan who was diagnosed with schizophrenia—her father's diagnosis—a few months after the assault. "[The stabbing] was necessary," she says in one video-recorded interrogation. Unlike Anissa, who cries and wraps her arms around herself in the interrogation room, Morgan's affect is flat. She doesn't cry at all.

On Friday, September 22, ten of twelve jurors voted that Anissa, now fifteen, was not criminally responsible. She is in a state mental hospital and could be released in three years or up to twenty-five years. The *Milwaukee Journal Sentinel* reported on October 5 that Morgan, also fifteen, had agreed to plead guilty in exchange for a deal acknowledging her lack of criminal responsibility due to mental disease. She, too, was ordered to be committed by the Department of Health Services—in her case, for as long as forty years.

One could say of my younger self that she was simply highly imaginative. Spirited. Already prone to storytelling, which would make sense for her future self—the novelist, the writer. Children are prone to believing in the things that they pretend are real; how many, for example, genuinely fear the boogeyman under the bed, or the monster in the closet? How many really do see ghosts in their rooms that they swear are real?

If Anissa and Morgan had never attacked Payton Leutner, they might not have been diagnosed with any form of the schizophrenias as preteens. They might have been called cheerful, spirited, and highly imaginative until some future year, in which they wandered into a fracturing of their realities that could not be denied. In the absence of their friendship and its shared delusion, or in the absence of the Creepypasta Wiki and its scores of pictures, videos, and other documents about the Slender Man, their mutual tendencies toward instability might have pulled them in less-dark directions. As I was, they might have been diagnosed in adulthood. They could have learned to deal with the schizophrenias. Hopefully, they still might.

Reality, On-Screen

The action-thriller-sci-fi movie *Lucy* was released on a Thursday in July 2014. Luc Besson's film is based on the premise that Lucy, played by Scarlett Johansson, is unexpectedly bestowed with the ability to use up to 100 percent of her brainpower, not the 15 percent with which most humans operate. This ability gives her superpowers and, ultimately, the wisdom with which to direct humankind. Before its release, *Lucy* had already received plenty of praise, though I told my husband, C., that I wanted to see the film even if it was a critical flop—for months I'd been making open-mouthed faces at him when the trailer appeared, punching him in the arm as Lucy dispatched thugs with a flick of the wrist, or as Lucy walked through an airport, her hair morphing from blond to black. We bought tickets for a Friday showing.

Four of us saw *Lucy* at the Metreon in San Francisco that day: C. and I had invited our friends Ryan and Eddie, who excused themselves from work to come. I'd learned a month earlier that Eddie had been diagnosed with schizophrenia more than a decade ago. I didn't know him well—he showed up occasionally at my house to play Dungeons & Dragons, and I recognized him as the heavily tattooed, and highly stoned, redhead we'd met at a balcony barbecue the year prior. He was the first person I'd knowingly met whose diagnosis also belonged to the collected schizophrenias. Still, Eddie and I had never spoken one-on-one about our diagnoses, or about our experiences with psychosis, and he wasn't exactly my friend but an acquaintance on the periphery.

I don't know at what point in the film *Lucy* became a problem for me. Ryan told me that during an early scene in which the drug-filled bags in Lucy's abdomen burst, and she begins to violently experience the transformation from ordinary twentysomething to superhuman entity, he almost reached over to ask if I was okay. Ryan, whom I consider a brother, tends to have his fingers on the pulse of my mental state more attentively than anyone else does, and has sometimes pointed out mania or depression before I realized they'd come to call. I do know that at some midway point in the ninety-minute film, I pulled out my emergency medication, intended for encroaching psychosis, and gulped it down with C.'s Cherry Coke. I considered leaving, but wanted to see what would happen to Lucy. I'd taken the emergency dose because I felt myself slipping, and sensed myself hurtling into the reality of the film, leaving my own behind. I could feel my brain twitching with the belief that I, too, was gaining access to more of my brain than that of ordinary mortals, and that if I tried, I could destroy objects with its power. When *Lucy* ended, I stood and blindly shoved past the other three in the darkness.

Eddie and I were the first of our group to emerge into the corridor. I said to him, trying to keep my voice light, "Are you having as much trouble as I am right now?"

He answered, "Well, I do know that I'm using 20 percent of my brain."

In the film, access to 20 percent of one's brain enables echolocation.

During a psychotic episode the winter before, C. and I had watched *Doctor Who* together. By the time the episode ended, I was lost.

"Is it happening somewhere else?" I asked. "Did that just happen in another place?"

He explained the concept of television to me. The show had actors in it who also appeared in other TV shows and films. The actors had lives that had nothing to do with what happened in the TV shows and films. The actors lived in reality, which was different from the unreality of the TV shows and films. The TV shows and films were scripted by human beings, who also lived in reality, and who wrote stories that were then turned into TV shows and films. Those human beings were writers, like me. I remained distressed and confused until we put on *MasterChef*, a reality cooking show that more closely resembles the world that I was supposed to believe in.

But that incident happened when I was ill, during an episode of active psychosis. We intuitively knew, for example, not to watch *The Hunger Games: Catching Fire*, which was in theaters at the time—and which I'd been excited about seeing—because the world of *The Hunger Games* was not ours, and because the theatrical experience would be too immersive for my addled brain to handle. We understood that, faced with an enormous screen, and wrapped in a cocoon of Dolby Surround Sound, I'd likely become agitated. I'd believe in *The Hunger Games*. I'd worry about whatever District I believed myself to be in; I'd wonder whether I'd have the mental and physical agility to emerge as Victor. We'd decided to watch *Lucy* believing that I could withstand the force of its alternate reality.

I didn't always recognize the feeling of becoming psychotic, because I didn't always understand what it meant to *be* psychotic—but having found myself in that crumbling landscape again and again, I now know the signposts that precede my psychotic episodes. I cannot speak for people who may take a different route, or fly instead of walk, but the feeling of my mind entering a state of rapid fracture is familiar enough now that I can describe the terrain.

It's one thing to be able to say, "I saw blood dripping down the walls," or "The landlord has installed cameras in my apartment," but it's another to talk about how it feels under the skin to see and believe things that aren't real. I can rattle off the symptoms of a panic attack: shortness of breath, numbness in the extremities, a quickening heartbeat, feeling that death is imminent, et cetera, but there is no corresponding checklist for the sensations of psychosis. The list of symptoms for schizophrenia, the "prototypical psychotic disorder," includes delusions, hallucinations, and disorganized speech in Symptom Group I ("positive symptoms"), and apathy, lack of emotion ("negative symptoms"), and/or severely disorganized or catatonic behavior in Symptom Group II. These symptoms are largely observable by an outsider, which is fortunate for a clinician who might otherwise be faced with someone who is uncommunicative or nonsensical, and therefore hard to treat. A person experiencing psychosis can seldom describe the ongoing turmoil with any kind of eloquence, but they might be able to tell you what it was like in hindsight, when the damage is in the rear window.

Before the psychosis properly begins, as I experienced during *Lucy*, I experience an agitated sense of something being wrong. The wrongness isn't limited to the grotesqueries mutating inside, but is also true of the world at large: how did it get this way, and what am I supposed to do with it? I mean this not only of dailiness, which is full of restless hours that must somehow be spent, but also the sky, the walls, the trees, my dog, the windows, the curtains, the floor—all of which are but a small portion of everything that needs my attention, including everything abstract and concrete, even as my ability to deal with them is at first dwindling and then absent. The more I consider the world, the more I realize that it's supposed to have a cohesion that no longer exists, or that it is swiftly losing—either because it is pulling itself apart, because it has never been cohesive, because my mind is no longer able to hold the pieces together, or, most likely, some jumbled combination of the above. I can understand only one piece or the other, even though the sky is supposed to belong to the same world as the curtains, and the dog that enters the room draws my attention as an entirely new object to contend with. People write about the so-called comfort of being insane in the same way they cavalierly refer to the happy ease of being developmentally disabled, but in this liminal space I am aware enough to know that something's wrong.

Something's wrong; then it is *completely* wrong. After the prodromal phase, I settle into a way of being that is almost intolerable. The moment of shifting from one phase to the other is usually sharp and clear; I turn my head and in a single moment realize that my coworkers have been replaced by robots, or glance at my sewing table as the thought settles over me, fine and gray as soot, that I am dead. In this way I have become, and have remained, delusional for months at a time, which feels like breaking through a thin barrier to another world that sways and bucks and won't throw me back through again, no matter how many pills I swallow or how much I struggle to return. What's true is whatever I believe, although I know enough to parrot back what I know is supposed to be true:

these are real people and not robots; I am alive, not dead. The idea of "believing" something turns porous as I repeat the tenets of reality like a good girl. When hallucinating, the idea of "seeing" or "hearing" something is similarly untrustworthy. I'll see a thing well enough to duck or jump to avoid it. Still, I know what is supposed to be true, and that includes a reality without shadowy demons or sudden trapdoors.

Movies, to differing degrees, are made to enforce the stories they tell, and we applaud when such power is wielded efficiently. An Oscar-winning drama makes us cry, and earns our admiration, because we believe to some degree in the story on-screen; we make a pact with the film to suspend disbelief. If the story is absorbing and the director skilled, we allow ourselves to agree that the actor truly is abandoning his soulmate in a cave, and, accordingly, we ache if that actor is deft enough in his craft to make us believe his pain. His grief becomes, in a way, our grief—our pain at arm's length, but still close enough to make us wince. Even tearjerkers can be considered efficient, if only because their melodrama cuts straight to our softest places, and gives us the pleasure of plugging in to our own capacity for empathy, no matter how corny.

Film's technological progression, then, compounds whatever realism does exist. Sitting and watching a projected film with reels rattling in the background, or with an accompanying live organist pounding at the keys, is a different cinematic experience from that of watching a film on an enormous IMAX screen (IMAX's tagline, accordingly, is "IMAX Is Believing"). During an opening scene in *Lucy* that features the famous, prehistoric Lucy, I marveled at how agile computer-generated imagery (CGI) had become since *The Matrix*—a reality-buster that I saw at its release, and that I don't dare to watch now—not to mention the groundbreaking *Terminator 2* or

Jurassic Park. The Microsoft Home CD-ROM *Dinosaurs*, released in 1993, thrilled me as a child; watching its movie clips was my first experience of 3-D computer animation. But I wondered over the next twenty years, as CGI became increasingly prevalent, whether we'd look back at movies such as *The Mummy* or *War of the Worlds* and laugh at how easily audiences had been suckered by a technology still finding its legs. It's possible to find an online list of the "10 Most Unconvincing CGI Characters in Movie History" as easily as the "25 Greatest CGI Movie Moments of All Time." Prehistoric Lucy mutters, makes faces, and blends into an environment comprising elements that may or may not be constructed: a real or false river, a true or invented sky. I can't tell the difference.

The next morning, over breakfast, I asked C. if we could talk about *Lucy*. If we could figure out what caused my reality to falter, I said, I'd know which films to stay away from.

"Well," C. said, "Lucy would sound crazy under ordinary circumstances, because of the things she claims she can do. The trouble for you might be that she can actually do them." *Lucy* insists that my reality—and the reality of those around me, which I'm supposed to trust when psychotic—isn't true reality. The film goes forth to embellish, with vivid cinematic tricks, its definition of what true reality is.

The 2001 film *A Beautiful Mind* traces the life of mathematician John Nash, played by Russell Crowe, with an emphasis on the role of schizophrenia in Nash's relationships and work. In attempting to place the viewer inside Nash's "beautiful mind," Ron Howard resorts to Shyamalan-esque machinations, featuring a perplexing twist in which Nash's grim supervisor at the Department of Defense, as well as a longtime friend from Princeton and his charming niece, are—*ta-da!*—revealed to be figments. Psychosis is, in

A Beautiful Mind, nothing more than an intensified version of childhood's imaginary friendships, and goes on to haunt Nash even after his recovery; in the film's final scene, as Nash is awarded a Nobel Prize in Economic Sciences, he glimpses the three figments. Schizophrenia, the movie implies, is forever.

It's easy to criticize *A Beautiful Mind* for its hokey depiction of schizophrenia. In fact, I first saw the film shortly after its release, at a recommended showing held by my Abnormal Psychology class at Yale. The point was to show us how Hollywood gets psychosis wrong, but Howard's use of cinematic figments is less crude when seen as a metaphor for delusion. Supervisor William Parcher is technically a recurring hallucination—a trick of the senses that can walk and talk, courtesy of actor Ed Harris—but he's also the character who kicks off Nash's paranoid belief that he must crack an elaborate Soviet code in order to spare America from communists. Without Parcher's sinister presence, the viewer could never become complicit in the belief that Nash is tangled up in matters of national security.

Years later, I would experience my first hallucinations, which were nothing like the recurring figments Russell Crowe experiences in *A Beautiful Mind*. Not long after that came the delusions, though I am still waiting for my Nobel Prize.

I did see *Catching Fire* in a theater. I was no longer psychotic, and I'd secretly booked tickets for C. and me for a 7 p.m. showing. We sat in the plush seats of the Kabuki theater in San Francisco's Japantown and watched Katniss Everdeen fight for her life. One scene that particularly grabbed me involved a jabberjay attack; on her side of the force field, Katniss is swarmed by genetically modified birds, known as jabberjays, that weaponize through mimicry the sound of her sister being tortured. Katniss screams, agitated and panicking, as her companion Peeta tries to tell her that *it's not real*, but the invisible barrier keeps them apart. Despite his best efforts, she can't hear him explain. The scene felt like a metaphor for so many things.

Later, as we walked toward the parking garage, C. said, "Remember the jabberjay scene?"

I said that I did.

"It was hard to watch," he said.

In the theater, we had let the film wash over us, and yet my boundaries had been solid. I could engage with the film fully without being lost inside of it. When the lights came up, and the audience began to stir, I reached for C.'s hand as though we were any other couple ready to go home.

John Doe, Psychosis

Hallucinations

I used to see John at inopportune moments. This was most likely to happen in an unfamiliar city, where it seemed semilogical that I might run into him. He also appeared when I was close to home, including one night at a bar where I was supposed to be celebrating someone's birthday. Instead I spent the entire night staring at, and then following, a man who to my mind so closely resembled John that I couldn't look away. This doppelgänger was with a woman, and he laughed with his arm around her, a glass of brown liquor in one hand. I escaped the bar and stood on the sidewalk, shaking, but continued to watch him through the open door.

The incident at the bar occurred in 2006. John was my boyfriend in high school, a bit less than a decade prior. I had broken off communication with him in 2003.

This sort of mirage is not uncommon among abuse and rape survivors. There are online forums for rape survivors where people say things like "So i sit in my apartment where i was almost kiled [*sic*] 2 years ago. I still see the blood stains," and "Its [*sic*] weird but sometimes i can still smell him . . . im [*sic*] scared to go to sleep." Both women state, as if in chorus, "I see his face everywhere." There are the films where a woman is walking home from work, milling through a swarm, and there he is. She panics, looks again—it's a kid who can't be more than twelve, or a CEO-in-training who looks nothing like the shark-eyed predator from her cinematic flashbacks. The phenomenon indicates preoccupation. It's the reason Chris de Burgh croons about seeing his (purported) lover's face everywhere. I'm not thinking about him, but I'm thinking about him. He's waiting at a broken-down, torn-up gas station in the shittiest, most deserted part of my mental geography: roll up your windows, lock the doors. John's the reason that I'll suddenly and repeatedly smooth down my husband's hair while looking up at him in bed: because his face has mutated, and adjusting his hair is the only thing that can stop the visual disturbance.

In Jen Percy's book *Demon Camp*, her chronicle of a soldier's life after war, an unnamed neuropsychologist tells her about the neurological consequences of trauma: "Sometimes the amygdala enlarges, the hippocampus shrinks. Trauma can cause inflammation, atrophy, neuron death, and shrinkage. Parts of the brain can wither, rearrange, and die." It's also commonly believed that the brain suffers physiological damage because of schizophrenia; according to one 2013 study, the highest tissue loss occurs in the first two years after the initial episode, and though it may slow after that, the loss does continue. One might then suppose that the combination of trauma and schizoaffective disorder could cause a potent neurological time bomb.

I developed post-traumatic stress disorder in the spring of 2014. My understanding of PTSD was limited to anecdotes from a friend who'd been attacked in a war zone, and to the experiences of fictional characters; I thought my nightly chills and sweats, acute sensitivity to sound and smell, and other such physical torments were due to complications from chronic illness. But I began to have nightmares. I'd sit up in bed, shot through with terror, hyperventilating in the dark. Some nights, I could startle from anything—a dog barking down the block; the pronunciation of the word "elegant" in an audiobook. I usually startled up to twenty times a night, the hypervigilance increasing with each jolt until every inch of my body was reduced to raw nerve. I began to sleep sitting upright against the headboard, because being supine made my symptoms exponentially worse. I sent my psychiatrist an email. It began, *I think that I may live with some form of PTSD.*

Dr. M replied with an explanation of possible treatments, calling my experience "chronic PTSD": *Your case is much more complex because of the schizoaffective disorder, which I don't believe is secondary to the PTSD but is its own additional factor.* I'd been living with medication-resistant schizoaffective disorder prior to the new diagnosis, and PTSD, while uniquely excruciating, was not—unlike schizoaffective disorder—considered to be incurable. Dr. M encouraged me to seek trauma-specific therapy; because my symptoms were causing sleep deprivation, she also prescribed Intuniv, which is marketed as a nonstimulant treatment for attention-deficit/hyperactivity disorder, but also has an off-label use for hypervigilance and nightmares. I was grateful for these things—these new pills and new forms of therapy—and I was grateful for the hope of a condition I could eliminate.

My literary tastes changed. I began to read Jo Nesbø's thrillers, beginning with *The Snowman.* This novel, in which the titular serial killer tortures, mutilates, and kills women to build them into "snowmen," was the first I'd read of Nesbø's Detective Harry Hole series. I read the entire series. I listened to the audiobooks, lulling myself to sleep with descriptions of torture. I propped my phone on the sink so that I could hear autopsy scenes as I showered. The victims in these books, particularly the ones who endure the most grotesque violence, are almost always women.

But there were only so many of his books out there, and I needed to fill almost every waking moment with violence. I binge-watched *The Killing* and *Hannibal* and *The Fall*, which also meant rewatching particularly torturous episodes of *The Killing* and *Hannibal*; I listened to more audiobooks in the same genre, some written in such lousy prose that I believed I was killing off brain cells faster than either schizoaffective disorder or trauma could; I read Stieg Larsson's Millennium trilogy, and then I watched the movies in Swedish. It is impressive, and horrifying, how many authors choose to employ the trope of discovering a woman's body in pieces, scattered, or in garbage bags, unrecognizable. I wondered if bookstores, instead of having sections for Mysteries or African American Literature, ought to cordon off a section for Girls in Trouble.

Why was I doing this? Some PTSD sufferers consciously or unconsciously put themselves in danger to "fix" the original trauma. I decided that I was, in vicariously living through these girls and women, doing the same thing. Perhaps it was a kind of exposure therapy. If I could only experience enough violence, if I could only hear enough descriptions of women's bodies being found in pieces, I could convince my sympathetic nervous system to calm the hell down.

I experienced psychotic symptoms for the first time when I was a senior at Stanford. I experienced a series of repeated hallucinations of girls screaming for help outside my window. The first time it happened, I called the police, who came, and who, after searching, told me that there was no one there. The second time, I called my mother, who told me not to call the police again. She didn't say that the girls in trouble weren't real, but it's what she meant. They once appeared to me unbidden, demanding that I pay attention. Now I hunt them down. Now I seek them out.

Thought Disorder

EMDR, or Eye Movement Desensitization and Reprocessing, is one therapy frequently used to treat the psychological consequences of trauma. For a client to receive "true" EMDR treatment, as developed by Dr. Francine Shapiro, the clinician must adhere to the training guidelines and standards of either the EMDR International Association or EMDR Europe. Such training guidelines and standards may be found in Dr. Shapiro's textbook, *Eye Movement Desensitization and Reprocessing (EMDR): Basic Principles, Protocols, and Procedures*, which is presently fifty-nine dollars when purchased from emdr.com; *Getting Past Your Past: Take Control of Your Life with Self-Help Techniques from EMDR Therapy*, also by Dr. Shapiro, is a mere seventeen dollars on the same website.

The therapist who performed an ad hoc version of EMDR on me when I was in my early twenties had done so after telling me that I was "stuck." I didn't deny it then, and I won't deny it now. My relationship with John had ended years ago, and the capital-*T* Trauma of being raped and abused by him had happened years before that, and yet I was talking about him in almost every therapy session, repeating over and over variations of the same stories, unable to move past the topic to speak of present-day concerns. She suggested that we try EMDR. She wasn't trained in EMDR, she admitted, but she could learn for the sake of my therapy. I was willing to try almost anything.

The framework of EMDR is this: through eight phases of treatment, as outlined by Shapiro, the client will learn to process their trauma via assessing a target event and its concurrent pictures or scenes, exploring the cognitions behind the target, and performing eye movements as led by the therapist until their SUDS, or Subjective Units of Distress Scale, rating decreases to zero or near zero. In a Q&A conducted by the *New York Times*, Shapiro explains that "the goal is to let the brain's information processing system make new internal connections as the client focuses on the thoughts, emotions, memories, and other associations." In other words, thinking about other things while moving your eyes in a prescribed way rewires the brain. According to the therapy's origin story, Shapiro noticed while on a walk in the woods that her negative emotions decreased in severity when her eyes darted from side to side.

It is possible, according to the EMDR Institute, that clients may feel relief almost immediately.

I told a few people after my EMDR sessions that my "stuckness" about John had evaporated. It was as though, I said, parroting something I'd read about EMDR results, a photograph of him had gone from color to black and white; he was still there, but the saturation had gone down. In hindsight, I might have saved hundreds of dollars, and been equally affected, by purchasing *Getting Past Your Past* and trying EMDR on myself.

SUDS is a framework developed by psychologist Joseph Wolpe, but what are our experiences of disturbance if not subjective?

Not long before I finally stopped talking to John, a friend told me that a mutual acquaintance had claimed that she didn't believe I'd been raped.

"If she'd really been raped," the mutual acquaintance had said, "there's no way she'd still be talking to him."

SUD = eight: the beginning of alienation, approaching loss of control.

Delusions

In 2006, post-EMDR, I believed in the success of my treatment; the trauma had not been eliminated, but the wound was now scarred over. Eight years later, I came across the search for John Doe 28 via a tweet:

> The FBI is seeking the public's help to stop a child predator. pic.twitter.com/w3GzJ77Fya
>
> fbi.gov/news/st

The first time I saw this message, shared by a feminist blogger, I ignored it. But she retweeted the missive the next day, and the repetition was enough to cause me to click on the link. The article showed three grainy pictures combined into one JPEG: a close-up of a man's profile; another close-up of a man from the front, with a small figure in blue directly in front of him; finally, a close-up of the man's burgundy shirt, which had either a shark or a fish decorating the breast.

And then I said, "Fuck." Or perhaps I simply thought it while reading the FBI article about John Doe 28, whose whereabouts were unknown, and who was understood to be in his thirties or forties, with wire-rimmed glasses and a receding hairline. He was believed to be American because he utters a single word, "careful," in the child porn that bears his face. The John Doe 28 video was found during a raid on a home in San Francisco, which is where I live. The article was written by FBI San Diego, which is the city where, as of less than six months before I saw the tweet in question, I knew John lived.

Was it John in the video? I couldn't be sure. The image was grainy; the face wasn't quite right. I consulted with a friend about whether to act. I kept checking the image to see if it triggered gut-level familiarity or fear. I wondered if John would be the kind of person who would wear that kind of burgundy shirt. Would he own a shirt with a shark on the breast? I'd once gifted him a pair of hot-pink pants, which he wore until, according to him, his mother threw them away.

I called the FBI. It was similar to calling my cable internet provider: the Muzak was cheery; a recorded female voice told me that they valued my call and appreciated my patience. When someone did pick up, I told her what I knew, which was that an ex-boyfriend and registered sex offender resembled John Doe 28. She took my information. "We'll call you if we need anything," she said.

These days, I still check to see if John Doe 28 has been identified. I wonder how insane it is that I thought the two men looked similar enough to call the FBI, but there's no one that I can ask to make the comparison for me. When I suspect that I'm experiencing a hallucination, I might ask a friend, "Do you hear that?" Reality checks are a common tool for people with a psychotic disorder. Yet no one who remains in my life knows, or has ever known, what John looks like. I have wiped him out of my life in almost every way I can.

Catatonia

For years, I wanted to talk to my partner, C., about what had happened to me. He didn't want to hear about what had happened to me. I wanted to buttonhole people on the street and tell them my story. This was impossible to do, and inadvisable.

When I did talk about what happened, I found that I did so flatly, sometimes nonchalantly. I dated someone in high school. That person abused and raped me. Later he was arrested and jailed for possessing child pornography and attempting to seduce a minor, who was actually an officer of the law, causing him to become a registered Megan's Law sex offender. Finally, in 2003, I told him to leave me alone. But parts of the story are left out. I loved him, but he didn't love me at all. He took something from me, but I could have walked away. A fictional narrative is considered nuanced when it includes contradictions, but a narrative of trauma is ill-advised to do the same.

These days, I hesitate to say much about what exactly happened between John Doe and me. I have been told by people that I've made a fuss about nothing, thus compounding the trauma of hurt with the trauma of feeling like a crybaby. I don't chronicle the rape, because to do so feels like testifying before the reader, who is judge and jury, and I have had enough nightmares about inept and poorly received testimony to try. No one has to believe me when I say that it was bad, but I refuse to give the public that kind of ammunition in the first place. I keep it to myself now: the shine of the streetlight, the look in his eyes.

Impairments in Social Cognition

Once, John said, "I know what's wrong with me. I don't need to see a shrink to find that out." He pulled a small bottle of something liquid and herbal-looking out of his bag. "I'm taking this for it."

I was too cowed to ask what he was taking it for, and what he thought was wrong with him. My guess at the time was bipolar disorder, due to his moods—he had, for example, stopped during a walk, picked up a brick, and hurled it into a nearby window, then kept walking as though nothing had happened—but who knows what was, or is, the problem as he claimed it to be? What was it that caused him to do the terrible things he did? A letter I received toward the end of our communications included the line *I'm sorry for raping you.* In that letter, he blamed most of his behavior on drugs.

After we stopped talking, I learned from a mutual acquaintance that he finally went to rehab. Later, after his access to the internet was restored, I'd find him on his public Facebook page, where John wrote an expletive-filled rant about people who, to his mind, blindly trust the police and the judicial system, and use information from those sources to judge him and his life.

I was one of those unwanted people, of course, who paid attention to detail in his life.

He was sorry. He was not sorry. He was still angry, but now he was specifically angry at a community that could, if they Googled him, encounter a first hit that has the sub-headline, "Sex Offender Registry Information for [John Doe]," because Megan's Law has allowed the public to view such information online since 2004. His criminal record is immortalized and viewable to anyone with access to a computer. I have wondered at the justice of permanently marking a man who committed certain crimes in his early twenties. The Megan's Law website states, "The law is not intended to punish the registrant and specifically prohibits using the information to harass or commit any crime against a registrant."

I, on the other hand, was not angry, despite years during which a variety of therapists attempted to bring me to that point at which they believed I could begin to heal. Instead, I forgave John, believing that forgiveness would bring me peace. In late 2013, I emailed him after over a decade of silence. I told him that I was all right, and that I hoped that he was okay too. I told him that I believed we'd both been doing the best that we could with what we both had at the time.

John wrote back. He said that he was glad to hear from me. He'd wanted to apologize, he said, but he'd lost my contact information. He said that he truly wanted to stay in touch.

I asked a friend what she thought of this. "He may deserve to have a good life," Miriam said, "but he doesn't deserve to have a good life with you in it."

This exchange of forgiveness was before the PTSD began—before the nightmares and the unending waves of terror, and before I saw someone who looked like him in a notice from the FBI. Forgiveness, as it turns out, is not a linear prospect. Neither is healing. Both flare up and die down; so do my symptoms of schizoaffective disorder. I have tried to control these "oscillations," as my psychiatrist calls them, but what, if anything, can truly be controlled?

There are still nights when I feel myself on a knife-edge, when the terror of PTSD mingles with the trickiness of unreality. It spreads through me like ink-blotting paper, and then I am unpredictably vulnerable to all kinds of stimuli—movie trailers that both rub up against where I am raw, shocking me with adrenaline, and pull fiction into my sense of what is real. At this point I can sometimes do a decent job of keeping myself safe from these perilous circumstances. Watching *The Great British Bake Off* has been one way to both calm my terror and keep me grounded in what is real. C. is good at knowing when to suggest that we watch old episodes; we curl into one another on the sofa with our dog nestled against or between us, and we learn about how to make a stiff enough crème patisserie. I've learned about how difficult it is to integrate passionfruit or rosewater into a recipe without bollocksing up the whole bloody thing. Slowly, the world coheres into something more closely resembling reality. The possibility of terror remains nearby, but does not spike at the slightest provocation. At this point, I kiss him. I go to bed.

Half a year after I called the FBI, I was at the dining room table, reading, while C. fried eggs at the stove. Then he was shouting, cursing at an injury caused by what I later learned was spattering oil:

a simple mishap. Without thinking, I jumped up and ran. I opened the bathroom door. I shut myself inside, huddling by the toilet, half-aware of what I was doing and what was happening. He came in to tend to his burn; as the door opened, I scrambled on all fours past him toward the bedroom. I opened the bedroom closet, which was lightless and carpeted with unwashed clothes, and shut that door behind me too.

I had my phone with me there, in the pitch-black bedroom closet where I was hiding and beginning to cry, and with my phone I searched for John's email, which I read and reread: "Please, can we talk more? Thank you. Love, John." I didn't know why I was holding his message in my hand. I was searching for something that I'd lost, something taken. I was hoping to find safety, or something like it. He was somewhere else. I was, allegedly, free of him, and I was safe, but I'd lost faith in that delusion a long time ago.

Perdition Days

I write this while experiencing a strain of psychosis known as Cotard's delusion, in which the patient believes that they are dead. What the writer's confused state means is not beside the point, because it is the point. I am in here, somewhere: *cogito ergo sum*.

In October 2013, I attended a speakers' training at the Mental Health Association of San Francisco. As a new hire at the bureau, I would begin, in 2014, to deliver antistigma talks at schools, government agencies, and other organizations around the city. Part of this training included a lesson on appropriate language usage—to say "person with bipolar disorder," or "person living with bipolar disorder," or "person with a diagnosis of bipolar disorder," instead of "bipolar" as a predicate nominative. We speakers were told that we are not our diseases. We are instead individuals with disorders and malfunctions. Our conditions lie over us like smallpox blankets; we are one thing and the illness is another.

I had endured my longest period of psychosis earlier that year, from February through August, and after trying every atypical, that is, new-generation, antipsychotic on the market, I began taking Haldol, a vintage antipsychotic, which cleared my delusions until November 4. On that morning, I looked at the antique sewing table in my office, seeing red wood without totally seeing it, and felt the old anxiety of unreality. The full delusion would not come until a day later, but I knew what this meant; the past few weeks had not been simply feeling "scattered," as I repeatedly told others, but had been prepsychosis signals and warnings.

Such signals seem ordinary to other people, and were ordinary to me. I was unhappy with my studio, so I rearranged the desk and created an accent wall with wallpapered gold peonies. Other signals were more foundational to my concept of self and addressed existential queries, which might have been a more obvious sign of distress. I was unsure about my foundational values, so I reread Danielle LaPorte's book *The Desire Map: A Guide to Creating Goals with Soul*, and "discovered" my Core Desired Feelings; having connected with my Core Desired Feelings, I dutifully wrote them in multiple colors of Le Pen on a gridded sticky note for my Filofax. I initiated work with a friend and "functional Muse," during which I began soul-searching about my relationship with writing and art in general, referring repeatedly to the question "What is art, and what is its function?"

All of this made sense in hindsight, as much as anything could make sense. In past psychotic episodes, my response has been to desperately assemble rituals or structures that will somehow ward off the anxiety of a psychotic fracture, or Eugen Bleuler's "loosening of associations." To assemble the parts of my mind, which has begun to fall apart—to become "scatterbrained"—into cohesion.

But analysis didn't solve matters. Neither did the new dividers for my Filofax, or the five 2014 planners that I ordered, wrote in, and abandoned. Ritual, my therapist told me later, would help, but it was not the solution; there was no solution.

Cotard's delusion was first described in 1882 by Dr. Jules Cotard, who called it "the negation delirium"; few instances of the disorder have been discovered since. Case reports can be found here and there—the story, for example, of a fifty-three-year-old Filipino woman who had recently immigrated to the United States, who "[complained] that she was dead, smelled like rotting flesh, and wanted to be taken to a morgue so that she could be with dead people." What we do know about the disorder hinges upon the tiny number of cases that occur worldwide, best summarized in a 2011 review article by Hans Debruyne et al. in *Mind and Brain*.

Debruyne and his colleagues suggest that Cotard's delusion is related to Capgras delusion, which I have also frequently experienced. Both delusions are rare, and both affect the fusiform face area and the amygdala, which processes emotions. The normal emotion that I would feel looking at a loved one's face is absent. The person afflicted with Cotard's is unable to feel emotions about familiar faces. It is thought that with Capgras this lack leads to a conclusion that the person's loved ones have been replaced by doubles, and with Cotard's that the person experiencing the delusion is herself dead.

In *Scientific American*, Dr. James Byrne writes about Cotard's delusion, "As comical as it appears to be, it is obviously a manifestation of some deep-seated emotional issues or brain dysfunction." It is this flip attitude toward such delusions that results in headlines referring to an "invasion of the body snatchers" and "reverse zombie syndrome"—two pop-journalistic, unsubtle references to low-grade horror that have little to do with the actual terror of either of these delusions.

In episode 10 of the TV show *Hannibal,* titled "Buffet Froid," a young woman turns out to be the killer. It's Dr. Lecter who introduces Cotard's delusion to Will, the show's protagonist, and therefore to the audience: "Have you considered Cotard's syndrome? It's a rare delusional disorder in which a person believes he or she is dead. . . . Even those closest to [her could] seem like imposters." The killer, named Georgia, has suffered from Cotard's delusion for years, and tore the face off one of her victims, presumably to see what was beneath. At some point, when Will encounters her, he shouts, unhelpfully, "You are alive!"

In the beginning of my own experience with Cotard's delusion, I woke my husband before sunup. Daphne, our dog, stirred, began thumping her papillon-mutt tail against the bedsheets. I'd been in my studio, but now I was shaking my husband, and I was crying with joy.

"I'm dead," I said, "and you're dead, and Daphne is dead, but now I get to do it over. Don't you see? I have a second chance. I can do better now."

C. said, gently, "I think you're alive."

But this statement, of course, meant nothing. It was his opinion, and I had my solid belief. I can state that the sky is green, but will you see it as such? I felt buoyant with the belief that I was getting a second chance in some kind of afterlife—it caused me to be kinder, to be more generous. I wasn't irritated by problems with computer downloads. I was sweet to telemarketers. It was true that I was dead, but I believed that it made sense to playact normalcy, or rather, an improved version of normalcy, because of the additional belief that I was in an afterlife. According to the logic of my delusion, this afterlife was given to me because I hadn't done enough to show compassion in my "real" life, and though I was now dead, my death was also an optimistic opportunity.

I tweeted, *What would you do if you were actually dead, and the life you were living right now was your second chance?*

It was a good hypothetical question, the kind of thing that a self-development junkie like me was apt to mention. But for me, it was true. I stayed within that perception for a single day before the delusion dimmed.

Dr. M told me straightaway that we would not be adjusting medications. Increasing the Haldol, which had ended my prior psychotic episode, created the risk of severe anhedonia, as well as tardive dyskinesia, for which there is no cure. There would be no more trial-and-error merry-go-round of antipsychotics. Dr. L, my therapist, pointed out that delusions are harder to medicate away than hallucinations. My form of schizoaffective disorder was, Dr. M said, medication-resistant. Both agreed that the best course of action was for me to learn coping mechanisms and practice acceptance.

At some point, I stopped talking. I leaned away from Dr. M in the maroon velvet chair.

Because Dr. L was present via conference call, Dr. M reported, "She's frustrated," while I sobbed over the back of the chair.

Dr. M mentioned a Cognitive-Behavioral Therapy for Psychosis group. Cognitive-behavioral therapy (CBT)—also known as "therapy with homework"—operates on a systematized process of adjusting false cognitions and maladaptive behaviors. One favorite study, or series of studies, has shown that CBT can be as effective as antidepressants alone. Because of this, insurance companies love CBT; why spend years on the couch yammering about childhood and dreams, or paying for expensive drugs, when a dash of CBT could do the trick? CBT for Psychosis, as far as I gathered while crying, was designed to teach people who live long term with psychotic symptoms how to cope with them.

CBT for Psychosis may be a lifesaving program. But at that appointment, I was convinced that I was dead, and I didn't see how a technique built upon adjusting beliefs could help me extract myself from that conviction.

The prospect of any kind of therapy felt to me like a suggestion that I sit down and meditate in a burning building.

During previous episodes, Dr. M had suggested both hospitalization and electroconvulsive therapy (ECT). They were not mentioned now, presumably because neither made sense. Hospitalization and ECT are offered as options for the journey toward getting better, and I was not going to get better.

The questions instead became about percentages.

What percentage of my life was going to be spent in psychosis.

What percentage of functioning I could expect. What percentage of my life could be spent at 60 percent functionality, as opposed to 5 percent. Dr. L told me that it was "unrealistic" to believe that I would ever be at 95 percent, or 100 percent, again, which is excruciating for an overachiever to hear.

What percentage of insight I could expect.

No one could, or can, answer these questions, of course.

Other questions: if I am psychotic 98 percent of the time, who am I? If I believe that I don't exist, or that I am dead, does that not impact who I am? Who is this alleged "person" who is a "person living with psychosis," once the psychosis has set in to the point that there is nothing on the table save acceptance?

When the self has been swallowed by illness, isn't it cruel to insist on a self that is not illness? Is this why so many people insist on believing in a soul?

From my journal, a list:
    11:13 p.m.
    I am Esmé.
    I am a writer.
    I have been married since 2009.
    I have living parents.
    I have a brother, who is married.
    I am 5 ft. 4.
    I was born in Michigan.
    My birthday is June 8.
    Flowers I love: ranunculus, peonies, sweet peas, jasmine, anemones.
    If we had a girl, C. wanted to name her Magnolia.
    We had magnolias at our wedding.

I did ask for an ECT consultation, otherwise known as the treatment of last resort, because the delusion now showed a sinister face that I found untenable. Whereas I'd once believed that I'd been gifted an optimistic afterlife, this shimmering notion was quickly replaced by the idea that I was in perdition. In this scenario, I was doomed to wander forever in a world that was not mine, in a body that was not mine; I was doomed to be surrounded by creatures and so-called people who mimicked the lovely world that I'd once known, but who were now fictions and could evoke no emotion in me. I spent much of my time in catatonic psychosis, a form of agitation characterized by overactive movement or no movement at all, and I lay in my bed feeling psychic agony more excruciating than any personal experience of physical pain.

My choice of the word "perdition" is deliberate, because during this period of illness, I'd chosen to listen to the audiobook of Marilynne Robinson's award-winning novel *Home*. To purchase and then listen to *Home* involved some complicated decision making. I'd been advised by my therapist months earlier to avoid consuming fiction while delusional. This, after listening to the audiobook of *The Yonahlossee Riding Camp for Girls* by Anton DiSclafani had me disoriented and believing that I rode horses and was at a boarding school. Psychosis causes my reality to become a hodgepodge; the addition of fictional elements is more unnecessary fodder for the mix, and the content can make me more scrambled and agitated than I already am.

Yet I purchased the audiobook of *Home* anyway. It is one of my favorite books, and one of the saddest books I've ever read; I didn't care if I slipped into Gilead. I chose *Home* knowing that I would likely become merged with the fictional world there, and I did. I would leave my room surprised that I wasn't stepping onto Ames's front porch, which would have been no more or less surprising than walking out the studio door and watching Glory make breakfast for her self-destructive brother, Jack, who doesn't know how to love her back. If I were going to be lost and wandering, I'd rather be lost in Gilead than anywhere else.

But the reality of *Home*, which spends a good deal of time discussing the state of Jack Boughton's soul, also brought the notion of perdition to me. I had little familiarity with the Calvinism that marks Robinson's work. What I did know from *Home* was that Jack Boughton is interested in questions of whether he was born predestined for perdition. In one scene, Jack tells his sister, Glory, that he believes that their preacher father fears for Jack's unsaved soul. Jack is known for his exploits and sins, and tells Glory that he finally looked up "perdition" in the dictionary: "The utter loss of the soul, or of final happiness in a future state—semicolon—future misery or eternal death." He adds, "This does all seem a little cruel, don't you think?"

Cruel or not, I latched onto that word. Having never been Christian, I still saw myself as being a soul in a state of eternal damnation because I couldn't otherwise explain what had happened to me.

During the "perdition days," which had no rhythm to them, I could not summon the motivation to do anything. I would not eat. I often would not move. I would not attempt to read or answer an email or have a conversation, because there is no point in doing anything when in perdition. Instead, there is only horror, and an agitation that refuses to manifest physically for lack of motivation.

There was the question of what to wear to my electroconvulsive therapy consult, which would take place at the University of California, San Francisco. If I looked too pulled-together for the consult, I figured, I wouldn't be able to convey that most of the time I was suffering from psychic torture. If I looked like a mess, I might end up institutionalized, and I'd had enough experience with psychiatric hospitals to know that I didn't want or need hospitalization.

Unless I'm catatonic, I do wear red lipstick and Chanel foundation. I do have short platinum hair. I do wear eyelash extensions. I sometimes go for months without showering, but I do not look disheveled. Friends text me for style advice. I have modeled—not professionally, or well, but I have done it. I tend to look superficially good under bad circumstances.

Having lost thirty-plus pounds in the last year (forty, by the end of the following week), I'd adopted the hyperbolically named "French ingenue" uniform. In what was a profoundly lazy, but effective, look, I shimmied into V-neck white T-shirts and black pants, or the same V-neck T-shirts and a black pencil skirt with calf-high socks. I sold or donated everything else, much of it acquired when I was a fashion writer and still holding down a full-time job: a flutter-sleeved, button-down Sonia Rykiel dress I'd bought and worn at a writing residency in Toronto; two differently sized, but otherwise identical, silk Marc Jacobs dresses; black pleather leggings that I wore as pants. To the consult, I chose to wear the pants and shirt. I put on makeup. I say that I put on the pants not because I remember wearing them, my memory being largely demolished because of psychosis, but because it was probably too cold to be wearing a skirt in that part of the city.

On the day of my consult, I helped C. back the Ford out via hand gestures from the sidewalk. As I leaned against a parked car, hand up, two young men walked by. The attractive, curly-headed one turned his head as he passed. Yes, I thought, our eyes meeting, you may think I'm hot, but I'm also a rotting corpse. Sucks to be you, sir.

I'd sold an enormous number of possessions in what I called a pay-what-you-want garage sale a few weeks before. C. had seen my tweet, and its link to my Craigslist ad, the day of, and called me about it. Everyone knows that giving away possessions is a potential red flag for suicide. I was already dead, so suicide never came to mind, but the idea of having meaningless possessions did. This unnerved the people who came to my pay-what-you-want endeavor, who didn't understand the concept of someone who wanted to sit there and watch people offer whatever they wanted, including nothing, to take away her things. Everyone asked, sometimes repeatedly, what amount I "intended" to sell, say, an elaborately knit cowl-neck scarf for. And I had no answers for them. One dollar was the same as ten dollars was the same as nothing. Some people seemed so confused by this that they just left. One woman grabbed armfuls of things and threw a five-dollar bill at me.

The only thing left afterward was a red cardigan. I left it in a bag and put it outside, but no one took it. When C. finally noticed the cardigan, he said, "But you love that cardigan."

Did I love that cardigan? I couldn't tell if I loved him or my mother, let alone a cardigan that I'd worn around my studio for a year. I threw the cardigan away.

The ECT consult was with a psychiatrist named Dr. Descartes Li.

"Naming their son Descartes," I said to C. "That is so, *so* Asian."

His office was much less terrifying than the hospital in which it was located. Later, C. would tell me that when he realized it was a psychiatric hospital, he'd immediately begun creating an escape plan to the car in case we needed to "make a break for it." I am perversely thrilled that even though he has never actually had to stay in a psychiatric hospital, he has been secondarily traumatized enough that a 1970s decor with odorous carpet and furniture, plus random amounts of incoherent yelling, will trigger his instinct to run in the opposite direction.

In the office, C. told Dr. Li that he liked his armchair. As he said this, I noticed the obvious stains on its surface, and wondered why C. had chosen that particularly disturbing thing to compliment (were those sweat stains from frightened patients or distraught relatives over the years?). Dr. Li had a copy of *Marbles: Mania, Depression, Michelangelo, and Me*, a recently released bipolar-memoir graphic novel, in a basket on top of his bookshelf, which I pointed out. No, I said, I didn't like it, but it might have been because I wasn't a fan of the art.

I had sixty minutes. How much of it was small talk? He asked for my psychiatric history, though he had much of it already due to thorough notes from Dr. M. There was no clock in the room. I didn't know how much to tell or what to leave out.

Pacing, they told me at graduate school, is one of the beginning writer's biggest challenges, because a beginning writer wants to tell all the wrong things, or everything at once. A nurse told us at the hospital in Covington, Louisiana, where I'd been committed during a Christmas vacation at my in-laws', that we were there because we did not believe in Jesus, a conviction that he had extrapolated from one young woman's confession of unbelief during group therapy. In October 2013 I was told that I fainted on a plane and went in and out of consciousness for four hours, that I might have had a seizure, that I had not had a seizure, that there was nothing to be done. I was told to go home and return to the emergency room if I fainted again. I was given a neurotransmitter test and told to mail it in, which I ultimately did not do, in part because of the remarkable number of misspellings and grammatical errors in the instructions, and in part because Dr. M told me that such things were hogwash. I was told that I had lost twenty pounds in two weeks, but that the only physical problem with me was peripheral neuropathy, or a numbness and prickling in my hands and feet, which was determined in October to be the result of a vitamin B6 toxicity, a determination to be rejected later. I was told that my debut novel was "still under consideration" at every house it had been sent to, which meant essentially nothing. In October I began to fracture, but I did not recognize it as fracturing, and I was told so many things that month, but I was not told that I was losing my mind again.

A side effect of my condition was a lack of interest in food or forgetting to eat it, leading to weight loss. In late November 2013 I was fitting into size XS tops and size zero dresses again. I surprised myself by the swiftness of it.

When I did look in the mirror, a practice that I generally avoided—the neurological disruption that creates a disconnect be-

tween emotional recognition and faces extends to my own as well—
I noticed that my body had changed dramatically. During one bathroom visit I lifted my bra, which had become baggy and sad. Bones.
Someday: ashes. I ordered a new bra, which was black and edged in
peach lace.

It arrived. I slipped it on. It was, somehow, ridiculous in its sexi-
ness. The cups barely covered. The straps were designed to look
like a harness. It was me, but it also wasn't me. I took a self-portrait
with my 1970s Polaroid camera. The resulting picture, in which I am
doing my best to make a charming, alluring face, I gave to C.

Somatic details figure heavily in these recollections: what I wore,
what I looked like. I told myself, through mirrors and dressing up and
Polaroids and weighing myself, You have a body. The body is alive.

But the more that I tried to remind myself of the various ways
in which I did, in fact, seem to have a body that was moving, with a
heart that pumped blood, the more agitated I became. Being dead
butted up against the so-called evidence of being alive, and so I grew
to avoid that evidence because proof was not a comfort; instead, it
pointed to my insanity.

Why do any of these things? Why did I behave in the manner of
someone who was alive when I believed, to differing levels of abso-
lutism, that I was dead? The notion of perdition never left me when
I was suffering from Cotard's delusion, but the degree to which I
despaired about it did. Most of the time, I could stuff down the despair far enough that I continued to—pointlessly, in my mind—
brush my teeth, sometimes wash my hair in the sink, and report my
symptoms to the phantom who claimed to be my doctor.

Suicide was not on my mind, though it had been before, during
my depressions. Perhaps if I'd considered suicide as an option, I
wouldn't have continued to do what I saw as meaningless tasks, and
would have tried to kill myself instead. But as a dead woman, my

condition meant that a successful suicide would simply doom me to the same thing, or to a deeper, unfathomably worse circle of hell.

Instead of killing myself, I watched the Adam Sandler movie *Funny People*. I was unaware of the fact that singer-songwriter James Taylor has a cameo in the film. When he came on-screen, I thought, without self-consciousness: Oh God. I can't believe that James Taylor is still alive, and I'm dead.

November 24, 2013

Like a child asking for a bedtime story, I left my studio and crawled into bed with C. at six in the morning. I said, "Tell me about what is real."

I asked him about everything. I asked him to tell me who I am, what I like, where I am from, what I do. I asked him about my parents. I asked him if they are real, even though they live in another country, and I only see them once a year. I asked him about the president, and about the vice president. He told me about our house. He told me about our neighborhood and the city in which we live. He explained where the furniture was from. That I'd picked out all of it myself. He told me about the farm table in the dining room.

I listened as he employed logic to tell me that I was alive.

"When people die," he said, "they are buried, and then you don't see them again. That's what happened to Grandpa this year. I don't see him anymore, but I see you."

None of this solved the problem, but it did help. It was as comforting as a bedtime story would have been. I thanked him. He went back to sleep, and I went back to my studio.

According to Greek myth, Demeter calls forth Persephone from the land of the dead once a year. I imagine myself as that pale daughter, who, in my imagination, has become so accustomed to being among the dead that she doesn't comprehend her transition into the land of the living. For me, the Cotard's delusion lifts without fanfare. There is no moment when I look around myself and realize that I have been resurrected, no shock of joy for having emerged from perdition. I have become sick with other, more definably physical ailments. I undergo neurological exams and MRIs and CT scans for cancer, and I am afraid, but I am conscious enough to know that there is no hope even of death in perdition, only more of the same awful suffering. It stands apart from loss, injury, or perhaps even grief, all of which are terrible, and yet are still beautiful to the dead woman, who sees them as remarkably human, and alive.

L'Appel du Vide

Francesca, when did you discover that you were an ambitious woman, and how?

When did your mind begin to turn on itself?

When did you realize that these things would make your life as an artist even harder than it would be otherwise?

I visited SFMOMA's Francesca Woodman retrospective—the most comprehensive exhibition of her work until then—in early 2012. The height of my Woodman obsession had occurred when I was much younger than twenty-two, the age at which Francesca Woodman had jumped from a window and died. By the time I went to see her photographs in person, I was twenty-eight; it was the winter that I was involuntarily hospitalized in rural Louisiana. It was the winter that I was in an outpatient program in San Francisco while trying to keep my full-time job.

Woodman is best known for the self-portraiture that she created as a student at the Rhode Island School of Design. Common motifs include nudity, reflections, blurred motion, and the decrepit settings of her *House* series. She is under things and behind things, part of the scenery (wallpaper, fireplace), distorted, long-haired, and pale. It's hard to see her face. At the exhibition, I was surprised to hear her recorded voice, which was unmemorable to me, and there was video, which I hadn't been expecting; prior to the retrospective, Woodman had existed for me only as a wraith in black and white. In the exhibit—held in a sterile museum, with standard white walls and plenty of empty space—she came across as cannily ambitious, and fully aware of her own gifts.

"The painter constructs, the photographer discloses," says Susan Sontag in *On Photography*. I could examine Woodman's carefully managed self-portraiture to suss out what lies below the surface of her images, and to try to uncover where one can spot the threads of her suicide, like gold glinting in an otherwise-dull tapestry. Suicide demands a narrative, but rarely, if ever, gives one. "Teen Kills Self after Parents Forbid Black Nail Polish," read one puzzling headline from my childhood. Why black nail polish? Why suicide? I didn't understand the self-destructive impulse then, but I did later. At fifteen, I kept a list titled "Reasons to Kill Myself" in the back of a journal, perhaps because I understood that a single reason was insufficient. According to one newspaper, Woodman jumped because she was frustrated by her lack of recognition: "Young Genius Kills Self after Provincetown [Fine Arts Work Center Fellowship] Rejection." (Which was, of course, itself a form of recognition.)

At sixteen, I was chosen to attend a summer program at the California Institute of the Arts, which also made me a California Arts Scholar in the field of creative writing. On the first day of the program, a man stood at the head of the room and unfurled a scroll of names before us: these were the people who had not made it into the program. The following year, in another summer program for the arts where I studied printmaking and drawing, I met a dishwater-blond named Clare who would become my best friend. Clare, I learned, was one of those people who had been on the CalArts scroll the previous year.

I hung my California Arts Scholar medal on a bulletin board in my bedroom, next to a strip of film from the beginning of *Eyes Wide Shut*. But I am constantly misplacing various symbols of achievement—I have no idea where my diplomas are, or the medal, though I continue to strive for more achievements, and more honors. In exercises designed to discern my primary values, *recognition*, to my dismay, appears again and again. I care about recognition as much as I care about my own self-regard, in large part because I don't trust my self-evaluation. I was obsessed with the boy who gave me the film strip from *Eyes Wide Shut*, but I can't imagine whether I would have felt the same way if my feelings for him had been requited. ("We mistake just feelings as feelings for love," a friend once told me.)

Woodman was always, her friend Giuseppe Gallo said, single-mindedly thinking about photography. Never distracted. "Every moment of Francesca's life," he said, "was in preparation for a photograph." One is more easily prepared with an always-ready model, and what subject is more available for exploration than the self? What better stuff to make art of if one is an ambitious artist, which Woodman undoubtedly was? Why not, as a writer, create essays in which I myself appear?

Francesca, what do you think of these photographs?
Do you see what I was trying to do?
I was trying to make myself more real.

During one psychotic episode, without a strict concept of myself or of the world around me, I coped by shooting with an SX-70 Polaroid and a Contax T2 camera. It was essential that the process involve physical film. Even better, instant film meant a tangible and immediate result.

Again, from *On Photography*: "All photographs are *memento mori*. To take a photograph is to participate in another person's (or thing's) mortality, vulnerability, mutability." To take a photograph, in other words, is to participate in one's own reality, to be a true member of the world of things. I taped a photograph to my wall; the photograph, which is of the back of my own head, surprised me because I'd forgotten about the birthmark on my neck—a dark brown and smudgy spot exposed by my chronically short hair. To have that mark turn up in a photograph was evidence of a self I remembered. I hadn't, in my psychosis, forged proof that I was the woman everyone else claimed me to be. After all, the birthmark is a classic signifier of identity. In the Grimms' tale "The Master Thief," it's the bean-shaped birthmark on his shoulder that convinces the master thief's parents that their son has returned. Even more fundamentally, a birthmark implies that I was once born—that I haven't always been here. A birthmark signifies one's entrance into the world.

Self-portraiture provides a certain notion of myself. Almost all the self-portraits I take during severe and prolonged psychosis are blurry and out of focus. Unlike Woodman, I don't try to create this effect, which happens because I must estimate an accurate focus before stretching my arms out in front of my face. The self-portraits are difficult to parse; they capture facial expressions that make me cringe later, when I see them in lucidity, because I don't recognize them, and because they are ugly in their attempt to approximate grins. When I examine them now, I wonder *why*. Why did I cover my face with my hand, particularly when I couldn't see my face in the lens? Why the grimace? Who is that performance meant for? Jackson Pollock said, "I am interested in expressing, not illustrating my emotions," but I look at those pictures and see anything but expression. Instead, there is an approximation, or an illustration, of what I believe an emotion should be.

Other self-portraits are shadows—my shadow rising against a hot wall by the butcher's, or against a cardigan slung over the back of a wooden chair. My mother-in-law told me one Christmas, after another episode of psychosis, that I was like Peter Pan: "You've just lost your shadow, and you'll find a way to stitch it back to your foot." I marveled at the congruency between that familiar story and the belief that, in death, the soul leaves through one's feet. I wondered if I'd literally lost my soul as I photographed the silhouetted marks that my body left on the world. The body was there, but something else—something essential—was missing.

When commenting on my ability to function, many point to my first novel as evidence of what I've managed to do despite being sick. This does not comfort me, because though I was depressed, often suicidally anxious, and periodically psychotic, in hindsight I call the author of *The Border of Paradise* a woman who was mostly well. I would have disagreed with this evaluation at the time, but back then I wasn't aware of just how unwell, both mentally and physically, I could possibly be. Rebecca Solnit says in *The Faraway Nearby*, "There is a serenity in illness that takes away all the need to do and makes just being enough," which has not been my experience. After all, prolonged and chronic illness stitches itself into life in a different way than acute illness does. With chronic illness, life persists astride illness unless the illness spikes to acuity; at that point, surviving from one second to the next is the greatest ambition I can attempt. The absolution from doing more and dreaming big that I experience during surgeries and hospitalization is absent during chronic illness.

During the worst episodes of psychosis, photography is a tool my sick self uses to believe in what exists. The photographs become tools for my well self to reexperience the loss. They are a bridge, or a *mizpah*—a Hebrew noun referring to the emotional ties between people, and especially between people separated by distance or death—between one self and the other. The well person has the job of translating the images that the sick person has left behind as evidence.

There are perhaps a hundred photographs that I've taken in periods of psychosis. I've shown very few of them to other people. One particular winter's worth of images is especially hard for me to sort through, and I consider those photographs to be a peculiar example of what memory can, and cannot, accomplish. I look at those images of the Christmas tree farm, and am immediately thrust back into that place and that time. The anxiety that pervaded those days returns. My body reacts with a fist in the solar plexus and tingling extremities. It reexperiences not the exact psychosis, but the terror that came with the psychosis, much in the way long-faded scars reemerge on my body under stress as ghostly memories made plain.

But there is much that I don't remember of the wreckage, which I see only now because the woman from the land of acute illness snapped photographs as souvenirs and keepsakes, including portraits of C. in which he is looking into the camera with exhaustion in his thick-lashed eyes and unkempt facial hair. I can't bear to look at those images now. I don't need to, because I can see in my mind's eye the despair in his face. I interpret those pictures of C. as a message of something that I couldn't see at the time: a missive delivered via the impartial camera, delivered from an external source that wanted me to see how the schizophrenias had damaged the great love of my life.

I would rather die young leaving various accomplishments, i.e. some work, my friendship with you, and some other artifacts intact, instead of pell-mell erasing all of these delicate things.

(Said Francesca in a letter.)

But, Francesca, what would obliterate those things in life?

Woodman was twenty-two when she jumped. Critics speak of what she might have done if she'd lived. When an artist dies, the art that never was is often mourned with as much grief as—if not more grief than—the individual themself. The individual, after all, was flesh and blood. It's the art that's immortal. Woodman's body of work, experienced in a museum setting, feels abbreviated. You walk through the final room and find the exit, expecting more.

What did Woodman mean when she suggested the destruction of work, accomplishments, friendships, the "pell-mell" erasure of those things called "delicate"? Beautiful things can be destroyed because they're obliterated by something else: the ordinariness of an artist's life is eclipsed by their manner of death. The obliteration can also be gradual. "It's better to burn out than to fade away," explained Kurt Cobain in his suicide note. He was a twenty-seven-year-old rock star when he shot himself, but his death made him an icon. Woodman and Cobain are frequently described as geniuses.

Are you in danger of harming yourself or others?

Do you have a plan?

When I was a lab manager, I was trained in the clumsy art of creating a suicide-prevention contract with potential or current subjects. The contracts were printed on half sheets of white paper. The subject-to-be had to agree not to harm themself. The subject-to-be had to also agree to dial 911 if they felt in imminent danger of doing so. I never had to create such an agreement, but I did wonder about its effectiveness. Was the suicide contract for our behalf or for the subjects'? Were we simply trying to feel as though we were doing something?

I once attended a meeting at San Francisco City Hall at which people were debating whether to install a "suicide net" beneath the Golden Gate Bridge, which would hopefully deter the suicidal and catch attempted suicides. The documentary *The Bridge* (2006) follows a year of suicides and suicide attempts occurring from that iconic bridge—twenty-four known suicides in all, and many more attempts. A common argument against the net had to do with the aesthetics of the bridge, the familiar silhouette that would be hampered by that kind of addition. I was in favor of the net, but had no idea whether its installation would result in fewer suicides in San Francisco, or even fewer incidents of Golden Gate Bridge jumping in particular. I'd convinced a member of the board to become pro-net by saying that because the bridge represented the possibility of suicide, its very existence therefore became a temptation. I compared it to my husband's former desire to have a gun in the house. If there were a gun in the house, I said, it would be both a temptation and a convenient means of suicide. In 2014, San Francisco voted on the installation of the net. Construction began in 2017 and is expected to be finished in 2021.

By installing the net, the city is saying that it is doing something about the tragedies that occur there. The net is a sort of suicide-prevention contract: *Look, we installed a net; we're holding up our end of the deal, so don't try it.* *The Bridge* was inspired by a *New Yorker* article by Tad Friend titled "Jumpers." Its concluding paragraph reads, "[To build a barrier] would be to acknowledge that we do not understand each other; to acknowledge that much of life is lived on the chord, on the far side of the railing."

Francesca Woodman was a jumper, though not an ordinary one. Most of the lives that end because of leaping from the Golden Gate Bridge are not the lives of famous people. They are not mourned publicly because of the loss of beautiful things that will never be created. No one writes in a magazine or newspaper that our culture is now poorer because those people have died.

Woodman insists in her letter that she would not like to "pell-mell [erase] all of these delicate things." What remains of her life are, as she calls them, "artifacts," because the life of breathing and heartbeats is the most delicate thing of all—which we all know, or all pretend to know.

I am older now by over a decade than Francesca Woodman was when she died, and older than I was when I saw the exhibition of her work at SFMOMA. I am still ambitious, but I must be careful about my ambition; illness has distorted my life such that it's become hard to recognize it as my own. On the phone in 2015 with my insurance representative, I learned that any mental illness is called a "mental nervous condition" under my plan; I stopped receiving disability benefits because "mental nervous conditions" are eligible for twenty-four months maximum. I marvel at how much illness I have experienced in these past five years due to late-stage Lyme disease, how the self before that time would be appalled to see the limitations of my life. All I can do is try to write well and pray to die peacefully. Francesca Woodman never has to watch her star fall, or to renegotiate her ideas of ambition, because she already faced her mortality, and is immortalized in her art.

Chimayó

When I walked into the neurologist's office in 2013 with C., it should have been apparent that something was very wrong with me. I struggled to keep open my eyes, not because of exhaustion but because of the weakness of my muscles. If you lifted my arm, it would immediately flop back down again as though boneless. My body frequently broke out into inexplicable sweats and chills. On top of all that, I had been experiencing delusions for approximately ten months that year. My psychiatrist suspected anti-NMDA receptor encephalitis, made famous by Susannah Cahalan's memoir, *Brain on Fire: My Month of Madness*, but that did not explain everything that was wrong with me, including the peripheral neuropathy that attacked my hands and feet, my "idiopathic fainting," or the extreme weight loss that caused suspicions of cancer—and so I was referred to this neurologist, who was described by my psychiatrist as "smart" and "good in her field."

"I don't think you have anti-NMDA receptor encephalitis, based on your chart," she said brusquely while C. and I sat in matching chairs that faced her examination table. "I'm doing this as a favor to your psychiatrist." And then she added, "Someday, we'll be able to trace all mental illnesses to autoimmune disorders. But we're not there yet."

In Santa Fe, New Mexico, where I had never been prior to 2017, my friend and fellow writer Porochista insisted that we visit the pilgrimage site of Chimayó. "You'll be able to write something amazing about it," she said. We were in the IV room of an integrative health care clinic when she said this, facing each other in enormous leather chairs with oxygen tubes in our noses and IV needles taped to our arms.

I did not feel like going anywhere. In that IV room I underwent several multinutrient drips and a few sessions of ozonated saline of differing concentrations, one of which made me so sick that I was moved to an expensive BioMat and handed two paper cups: one of tulsi rose tea and one containing a chunk of dark chocolate. Porochista and I were in Santa Fe for a nine-day round of medical treatments, and the combination of baseline chronic illness and intensive doctors' appointments, plus semiregular meals at restaurants, was nearly more than I could endure. To do anything more taxing than lying in bed brought on fevers and chills, nausea, dizziness, and difficulty breathing. This constellation of symptoms was, in Santa Fe, diagnosed as the result of dysautonomia, or, more specifically, postural orthostatic tachycardia syndrome (POTS). Porochista had been diagnosed with dysautonomia the previous winter, after she was sideswiped by an 18-wheeler; dysautonomia is also recognized as a complication of chronic, or late-stage, Lyme disease, the controversial primary diagnosis the two of us share.

"We can stay in the car," Porochista said about Chimayó. "Let's go and look around. We can see how we feel," she said, which was a common refrain during that trip, and is a common attitude among the chronically ill.

The neurologist I saw in 2013 ordered tests. I had an MRI and an EEG. Someone in a basement laboratory drew fifteen vials of blood, and after this succession of tests C. and I waited for the results, which could, depending, hurtle me toward an intimate knowledge of mortality, gift us with new diagnoses and possible treatments, or tell us nothing. By the end of it all, the most interesting finding from those blood-filled vials was the presence of antibodies for the calcium channel Ab P/Q type, which pointed to myasthenia gravis, Lambert-Eaton myasthenic syndrome, or cancer; however, both the MRI and EEG came back clean, which ultimately meant that the neurologist had no diagnosis for me. I continued to be aimlessly, miserably sick until I was diagnosed with chronic Lyme disease by a new doctor, through an IGeneX test in 2015.

Once I was diagnosed, the new doctor—known in the Lyme community as an LLMD, or a "Lyme-literate medical doctor"— told me that my diagnosis of schizoaffective disorder was likely related to an infection by *Borrelia burgdorferi* bacteria, and called my illness neuroborreliosis, which implies an infection affecting the brain and central nervous system. This would not be a diagnosis handed down by a doctor outside of the Lyme community, but I was willing to believe it. Until then, I had thought of my psychiatric illness not only as one of my primary identifiers, but as a beast all its own with an accompanying origin story. The narrative of bacteria infecting my brain suddenly turned my schizoaffective disorder into something organic—a problem amid a constellation of other problems, to be considered alongside my growing litany of symptoms.

A chronic Lyme diagnosis is a kind of belief system. I never experienced a tick bite that I was aware of; I'd had no classic bull's-eye rash. The Centers for Disease Control, which provides the framework from which conventional doctors across the country form their diagnoses, acknowledges that Lyme disease *exists*—in the 1970s, the citizens of Lyme, Connecticut, noticed a plague of medical symptoms, which were later pinpointed by Dr. Wilhelm Burgdorfer as originating from a tick-borne spirochete—but claims that "because of the confusion in how the term [chronic Lyme disease] in this field is employed, experts do not support its use." In other words: because Lyme disease may or may not be the answer for people who exhibit the symptoms of Lyme disease, and because "in many occasions it has been used to describe symptoms in people who have no evidence of a current or past infection with B. *burgdorferi*," the CDC errs on the side of dictating that chronic Lyme disease is not a valid diagnosis.

Because the CDC does not officially support a chronic Lyme diagnosis, the world of those who diagnose and treat chronic Lyme and those who are affected by the disease exists outside the parameters of conventional medicine. This world has a language, set of ideas, and arsenal of treatments all its own. Many LLMDs belong to the International Lyme and Associated Diseases Society (ILADS), which, according to its mission statement, is dedicated to "the *appropriate* diagnosis and treatment of Lyme and associated diseases" (italics mine). A cornerstone belief of ILADS and the chronic Lyme community is that the ELISA (enzyme-linked immunosorbent assay) screening test, which the CDC mandates as a necessary component of a true Lyme diagnosis, is unreliable and misses 35 percent of culture-proven Lyme disease. LLMDs instead use as their gold-standard a test from the aforementioned IGeneX, described as a "[Clinical Laboratory Improvement Amendments]–certified high complexity testing lab with expertise in testing for tick-borne diseases." Another ILADS cornerstone is that Lyme is "the great imitator," and is therefore often misdiagnosed as illnesses ranging from chronic fatigue syndrome (also known as myalgic encephalomyelitis) to amyotrophic lateral sclerosis.

To accept a chronic Lyme diagnosis is to adopt, at least partially, these beliefs. If you have the resources (financial, communal, cognitive, emotional, et cetera), you will seek out an LLMD and the treatments recommended by that LLMD, which means sinking a fortune into health care. I have yet to meet a chronic Lyme patient whose health insurance, if they are fortunate enough to have it, will cover their treatment for chronic Lyme—a lesson I learned only after gambling on coverage through my state's health exchange and being turned down time and again for reimbursement. Porochista told me that she has spent over $140,000 on treatment. A search for "Lyme" on GoFundMe turns up 51,366 results, including "Sarah's Battle with Lyme and Fibro," "Save Kaeley from Lyme Disease," "Help Aaron & Nicole Beat Lyme," and "Lessons in Lyme: Help Caden Smile!" The amounts being raised range from the thousands to the six figures for treatments that the CDC does not acknowledge or condone. To the CDC, these people are unfortunate, but they have no known recourse; they have fallen through the cracks.

I am someone who finds comfort in science and authority. After all, I used to work in a research laboratory, and while working at a fashion and culture magazine, I was derisively called "conservative" by the editor in chief during a botched pitch session. But to be so ill that I couldn't hold down a full-time job, and to simultaneously be without a diagnosis, treatment, or hope, made me receptive to the decree of chronic Lyme when my IGeneX test came back positive. Sick people, as it turns out, generally stray into alternative medicine not because they relish the idea of indulging in what others call quackery, but because traditional Western medicine has failed them.

For example, in discussing with writer Blair Braverman—a friend who has also been diagnosed with Lyme—an alternative, herb-based Lyme treatment known as the Buhner protocol, I learned that Stephen Buhner compares chronic Lyme to Morgellons. Morgellons is the creepy-crawly disease Leslie Jamison writes about in her award-winning *Harper's Magazine* essay "The Devil's Bait." Jamison is far from unkind in describing the people who believe themselves to be afflicted with Morgellons—a condition that allegedly causes crawling sensations beneath the skin and the emergence of colorful fibers from the pores—but the essay does make plain Jamison's belief that Morgellons is an illness of delusion. "They experiment with different cures and compare notes: freezing, insecticides, dewormers for cattle, horses, dogs," she writes. It's no wonder Braverman and I balk at the thought of being associated with such a thing. Then she sends me photographs of three pages from one of Buhner's books. According to Buhner, Marianne Middelveen, a microbiologist and medical mycologist, believes that the symptoms of a disease in cattle called digital dermatitis closely parallel those of Morgellons, right down to the lesions and "abnormal filament formation." Bacteria at the lesion sites are mostly spirochetes, just as are the Lyme *Borrelia burgdorferi* bacteria. But regardless of whether Morgellons is "real" or whether it originates from bacteria as Lyme disease does, I can no longer put myself at a comfortable distance from "those people" who self-diagnose with Morgellons. We are, in the end, linked by desperation based in suffering, and based on a system of conventional medicine that not only has no method of alleviating that suffering, but also accuses us of psychosomatic pathology.

When my LLMD, a man I'd been referred to by another doctor—
to whom I'd been referred by a Reiki practitioner/masseuse—said,
"You definitely have chronic Lyme," I was ready to believe him. Perhaps it's more accurate to say that I was ready to try to believe him.

For a year, back when my hallucinations and delusions were fairly
new, I considered becoming Catholic. This consideration was unrelated to the psychosis; I was engaged to be wed to a Catholic, and I
faced the question of conversion, which is mandatory for a Catholic
ceremony if both parties are not already part of the Church. Our
friend's wife, for example, had converted for our friend. At a bar
in New Orleans I peppered her with questions about how she'd
known it was the right thing to do. I should have realized before
asking that I would be dissatisfied no matter her answer; there is no
answer to that esoteric question that would help a questioning soul.

Still, I did what I had done all my life when faced with something
I did not understand: I read about it. I read Thomas Merton and
C. S. Lewis and *The Jesuit Guide to (Almost) Everything: A Spirituality
for Real Life* and the Holy Bible and guides to the Jesuit Examen and
Augustine's *Confessions* and Julian of Norwich's *Revelations of Divine
Love*. I went to Mass at the Catholic church down the street, where
I stood and sat at the appropriate times, sang along to "Gloria,"
and exchanged the sign of peace with my neighbors, though I never
gathered the courage to approach the sanctuary for blessing while
others, including C., took Communion. He and I had long conversations about God and faith—I was full of questions, and he answered as best as he could, sometimes pulling the New Testament
off the shelf for answers.

Catholicism appealed to me, and still does. The aesthetics of
Catholicism, which are rooted in mysticism and ritual, and which
often include Latin and incense and pillar candles, thrummed a chord

within my heart. I respected the intellectualism of the Jesuit tradition. And yet I would go to Mass, and I would hear the people around me recite by heart, in unison, the profession of faith, which began—

> We believe in one God, the Father, the Almighty, maker of heaven and earth, of all that is seen and unseen. We believe in one Lord, Jesus Christ, the only Son of God, eternally begotten of the Father, God from God, Light from Light, true God from true God, begotten, not made, one in Being with the Father . . .

—and I would wonder whether I could ever pronounce such things aloud, while boldly believing every word that passed my lips. I am certain that there are some people who convert without necessarily believing the entire profession, but I knew that I could not do such a thing, as it were, in good faith. In the end, I did not.

Chimayó is a town with a population of 3,170, and the El Santuario de Chimayó, which would be our destination, is a pilgrimage site where people pray for miracles, specifically miracles of healing. Built on the site of a miracle, El Santuario contains *el pocito*, a small pit filled with holy dirt described as having curative powers. A section of El Santuario's website, titled Testimonials, includes this: "I told her I'd FedEx her some holy dirt so it would get there in time. . . . The night before Ruby's scheduled surgery, Tony and Steve took the dirt and rubbed it on Ruby's body and prayed. . . . To their surprise the doctor came to them in the waiting room and said Ruby didn't need the surgery after all!" And this: "I will admit I was kind of scared at first, but my aunt and mother convinced me to not worry and to not be afraid. . . . I followed the steps and rubbed the dirt on the area of my legs where the pain was. . . . The next morning I woke up and felt little to no pain at all in my legs."

Illness draws me to places such as this. The prior winter, while visiting my in-laws in New Orleans, I had gone to St. Roch Chapel, which was built after Reverend Peter Thevis prayed to Saint Roch for his parishioners to be spared from yellow fever. The illness had been raging throughout the area, and Reverend Thevis found that his community was, in fact, miraculously saved. St. Roch Chapel has since become a place where those hoping for miraculous cures not only pray for intercession, but also leave behind symbols of their ailments as offerings once they've been cured.

The chapel was far smaller than I'd anticipated—smaller than any church I'd seen, smaller than a school cafeteria. There were no visitors or tourists save for C., his sister, her boyfriend, and myself. A statue of Saint Roch beckoned, colored in pastels. In a wide-brimmed hat, with a mustache and goatee, he looked a bit like a suave conquistador. Off to the side, in a closed-off, gated room about three feet by three feet in size, hung artificial limbs and crutches, as well as homemade plaques and miniatures of dogs, hearts, and crosses. These items serve as both decor and symbol; a glass eye is a glass eye, small and coated in dust like an outsize marble, but it suggests sight regained, suffering, and hope for any-one who notices it.

Hung on my bedroom wall is a quote attributed to Joan of Arc: "I am not afraid. I was born to do this." However my life unfolds, goes my thinking, is how I am meant to live it; however my life un-spools itself, I was created to bear it.

To the chapel I had taken a beloved stone striated by white lines. According to what I'd read, I was supposed to leave something only once I'd been healed—but my intuition told me to leave something then, and so I knelt and tossed the stone through the bars. I said a clumsy prayer while the sun sluiced through the windows into the tiny room. It is probably still there.

The belief that *DSM*-caliber mental illness might be linked to bodily illness, and particularly to autoimmune illness, as my neurologist proposed, is gaining traction. In the *Atlantic* article "When the Body Attacks the Mind," journalist Moises Velasquez-Manoff, author of *An Epidemic of Absence: A New Way of Understanding Allergies and Autoimmune Diseases*, describes the nightmare experienced by the Egger family when thirteen-year-old Sasha suddenly began to exhibit severe psychotic symptoms. One specialist diagnosed Sasha as having bipolar disorder, subsequently prescribing antipsychotics; Sasha's mother, who was a pediatric psychiatrist and understood the unlikelihood of a sudden onset of mental illness, persisted until she found a neurologist who suspected something else: an autoimmune variant of encephalitis. Upon infusion with antibodies used to treat autoimmune attacks, Sasha "improved almost immediately." "If an autoimmune disorder of the brain could so closely resemble psychiatric illnesses," Velasquez-Manoff asks, "then what, really, were these illnesses?"

According to the growing field of autoimmune neurology, the immune system can wage a misguided attack on a person's central or peripheral nervous system. My previously suspected diagnosis of anti-NMDA receptor encephalitis is one such example—the disorder occurs when the immune system attacks the brain's NMDA receptors, resulting in a chaotic array of symptoms such as speech dysfunction, hallucinations, delusions, and cognitive and behavioral disturbances—symptoms, in other words, that look like schizophrenia. In a 2006 study by William W. Eaton et al., which links three existing Danish data sets, the researchers concluded that "a history of any autoimmune disease was associated with a 45% increase in risk for schizophrenia."

Lyme disease might have escalated my existing psychiatric condition by triggering an immune reaction. Or, as my LLMD believes, Lyme might have directly infected my brain, causing the symptoms that led to a diagnosis of schizoaffective disorder. Perhaps I don't have chronic Lyme disease at all, but something else that may or may not be recognized by the CDC. For years, Dr. M implied that my disabling illness was the consequence of complex post-traumatic stress disorder, which I interpreted as a formal way of saying that it was all in my head, a form of hysteria. Most recently, she has tried to coax me into psychoanalysis, promising that she knows practitioners who have greatly helped their clients. Isn't it suspect, she asks, that I become exhausted after engaging in strenuous career-based activity? She supposes that this exhaustion is a type of punishing self-sabotage for any lick of success. These days, I tell people I have both chronic Lyme and schizoaffective disorder, and as far as I know, they believe me.

Porochista and I went to Chimayó on a Tuesday after IV treatment. An old friend of hers named Amy drove us, and they chatted as old friends do about the past and present while I sat in the backseat, watching the desert scroll by and worrying about how well my body would hold up—a worry that is daily and incessant in the face of whatever life demands of me.

This worry became inflamed when Amy parked the car and apologized for how far we would have to walk. Porochista, who used a cane as needed and had one with her throughout the trip, assured her that it would be fine, and I murmured assent, not wanting to voice apprehension to a woman who had played hooky from work to bring us to this holy place. We walked from the car to a path leading toward a collection of small buildings that made up El Santuario; on either side of the path were wire fences adorned with rosaries and crosses, bound and tied with twine or yarn to their links. The crosses were wooden, and often had names written on them, or messages such as PRAY FOR US MARY. Although it had been frigid for much of our time in Santa Fe, it was sunny when we arrived at Chimayó. I left my faux-fur pullover in the car, gambling that I wouldn't need it again—there was, after all, little chance I'd turn around and walk back to the car for it at any point.

In one long row of wooden stalls, people had affixed photographs of loved ones to the walls. A sign instructed that visitors pray for those whose images you saw there: people of all ages, genders, and ethnicities, including those who appeared hale and hearty, and those who were pictured in hospital beds with thin, pastel sheets pulled up to their bony chests. This collage reminded me of walking through Grand Central Terminal immediately after 9/11, when plaintive MISSING flyers were everywhere—overwhelming, futile sheets of paper emblazoned with the faces of the lost. And there were lost people here, too—photographs of soldiers who were POWs and MIA.

I snapped pictures with my camera. I took some on my phone. The wallpaper on my lock screen was of a Joan of Arc statue with the word "Hope" in gold across it. I saw El Santuario as being built on hope, which is not the same thing as faith. Hope is a cast line in search of fish; faith is the belief that you won't starve to death, or that if you do, God's plan could account for the tragedy. My morning prayers begin with, "Blessed Mystery, thank you for . . . and Blessed Mystery, may I . . ." Remission appears over and over in the latter: *May I be well.*

We walked among the little altars, leaves crunching underfoot.

Devotional candles, silk flowers, rosaries, and scribbled petitions were huddled around statues of Our Lady of Guadalupe and Our Lady of La Vang and a mosaic of Saint Francis. Carved above one statue were the words HAIL MARY FULL OF GRACE, THE LORD IS WITH THEE and DIOS TE SALVE MARIA, LLENA ERES DE GRACIA, EL SEÑOR ES CONTIGO. There was a shelter dedicated to local Native American communities, and there was Leona's Restaurante, which advertised Frito pies and nachos, but appeared to be closed.

The church itself is much smaller than almost any Catholic church I have visited, wooden and rough-hewn. Amy whispered that El Santuario emphasizes suffering and death as opposed to the resurrection, and it is true—a macabre Christ on the cross is marked with gaping wounds, and the Stations of the Cross are dark with violence in their depictions of Christ condemned. "Son though he was, he learned obedience from what he suffered," reads Hebrews 5:8. Believers, too, suffer, as 2 Corinthians 1:5 tells us that "for just as we share abundantly in the sufferings of Christ, so also our comfort abounds through Christ." I never did become a Catholic, but in my illness I became hungry to understand suffering; if I could understand it, I could perhaps suffer less, and even find comfort in the understanding. Books I consulted included *Man's Search for Meaning* and *No Mud, No Lotus*, which suggest, respectively, logotherapy and Buddhism. What I have found difficult is not seeking an escape hatch out of pain, whether that be pills, alcohol, or the dogged pursuit of a cure. In suffering, I am always looking for a way out.

And in the back of El Santuario, after soaking in the agony of Christ, we found the way out—the hope—the *el pocito* with a dirt floor, barely big enough for three people at a time to scoop out its miraculous holy dirt. It was the site where, a sign told us, the crucifix of the Lord of Esquipulas was found by Don Bernardo de la

Encarnación Abeyta in 1910—the miracle that birthed El Santuario de Chimayó. On the wall of the room sign read:

IF YOU ARE A STRANGER, IF YOU ARE WEARY FROM THE STRUGGLES IN LIFE, WHETHER YOU HAVE A HANDICAP, WHETHER YOU HAVE A BROKEN HEART, FOLLOW THE LONG MOUNTAIN ROAD, FIND A HOME IN CHIMAYÓ. —G. Mendoza

To remove the holy dirt, we used orange-and-black plastic children's shovels that were half-plunged into the pit. The dirt was more like silt, and sparkled in the sunlight that leaked in from a small window. None of us had brought a container, so we gingerly walked with the dirt in our cupped hands to the gift shop, where we bought decorative containers to take it home in.

Adjacent to one of Chimayó's many gift shops was a small museum. In this one-room museum I learned, through a large informational plaque, that in 1977, a twenty-one-year-old man named Jose Rodriguez carried a 250-pound, nine-foot-tall cross on a thirty-two-mile trek from the Rosario Chapel to Chimayó. When asked why he made the pilgrimage, Rodriguez responded that he was simply fulfilling a promise he made to the Lord three months prior. The promise itself was never reported, and neither was the outcome, if one was hoped for, of his journey, which is to say this: a young man walked a long way with a heavy burden to the site of a miracle.

Two weeks after I returned to San Francisco, my psychiatrist began the process of referring me to a medical specialist at Stanford. This was thanks to a research paper that my psychiatrist had come across in her studies, about another woman who also had antibodies for the calcium channel Ab P/Q type and symptoms of dysautonomia. Upon treatment with plasmapheresis, my doctor told me, the woman was cured, and so we began the long process of seeking my HMO's approval to send me to a doctor in the Stanford Autonomic Disorders Program, which is housed in the Neurology and Neurological Sciences Department at Stanford Medicine.

I was told that nine hundred pages of my medical records were sent to Stanford. In the referral authorization itself, I was listed as having two diagnoses: schizoaffective disorder, bipolar type and idiopathic peripheral neuropathy. There was no mention of fibromyalgia, complex PTSD, dysautonomia/POTS, chronic Lyme disease, or any of the other diagnoses I'd received over the years.

The possibility of uncovering something new thrilled me, and I anticipated the visit with fervor. By the time I saw Dr. J at the Autonomic Disorders Program, I was using a cane to help with fatigue and dizziness, and praying for some canny new insight. I hoped for a declaration. *Here it is,* he'd say, *the thing that's been undergirding your misery for the last five years.* And yet illnesses, like the geography of the schizophrenias, are hardly so simple. On a Tuesday morning, Dr. J finally examined me. He asked questions. He prodded and looked and ordered tests. C. and I went home feeling, as C. said, cautiously optimistic.

I received a lengthy report, which was addressed to my doctors, weeks later. Dr. J mentioned my LLMD, slighting him with the descriptor "who is presumably a Lyme specialist"; he had specifically told me at the office to seek no more treatment for chronic Lyme. The report prefaced every unusual finding with the word "surprisingly," as in: "Surprisingly, she had mild nystagmus," and "Surprisingly, she had increased glabellar reflex," and "Surprisingly, Romberg's was weakly positive to the right."

"Mrs. Wang has an interesting presentation," he said, and concluded with "It was good to see Mrs. Wang . . . I will be arranging communication with your office regarding her management, but will be happy to see her in the future if the need arises."

Hope, I write in my journal, *is a curse and a gift.*

The test results all came back negative. People congratulated me on this news, but I sought comfort in those who understood that negative test results meant no answers—meant Dr. J's diminished interest in my case and thus in my suffering—meant that I had no avenue of treatment to pursue and no kind of cure in my sight line. Ever since then, I have continued to experience monthly fevers and daily fatigue, as well as a constellation of other symptoms that have been brought to, of all people, a cardiologist. In the meantime, I am more well now in 2018 than I was in 2016, and more well in that year than in the four years prior to that one, which seemed to indicate something—but what, I am not sure. All I can do now is wait for spontaneous remission.

I take Haldol and Seroquel, two powerful antipsychotics that are either extraneous chemical additives or essential medications that keep me stable. I am not willing to experiment to see which. Haldol is not often taken these days, much as MAOIs (monoamine oxidase inhibitors) are profoundly less popular antidepressants than SSRIs (selective serotonin reuptake inhibitors); a GenX friend has told me that it is a "thing" now for millennials to abuse the newer, soporific drug Seroquel, which seems bizarre to me. I experience mild psychosis here and there, but do not consider it possible to ever be completely free of the schizophrenias. They have been with me for too long, I think, to be obliterated, unlike these more recent ailments, which feel like part of the wrong narrative, and make me wonder how many different types of sick girl I can be.

Beyond the Hedge

One winter morning I shuffled a deck of oracle cards with my eyes closed, and I realized that despite the blackness, I could still see what was happening in front of me. Here were the details of my hands, with the movements of each finger, every twitch of every narrow knuckle, made plain; I could see the cards, which were not clear enough to distinguish completely, but showed their blurry, colorful faces in broad strokes. I decided to further test this ability by holding colored pens, randomly chosen from a pouch, before my shut eyes. The pen test indicated that I could also "see" the colors behind my lids—imperfectly, yes, but well enough to grasp whether I was looking at a light color or a dark one, and I called out the hot-pink one immediately.

Journaling and drawing divinatory cards had become routine parts of my life earlier that year, when I was fighting psychosis and struggling to make the world cohere; I'd found that Tarot and oracle cards offered a decent framework from which to hang a fractured existence. Tarot cards vary from deck to deck, depending on the artist and/or creator, but typically follow a seventy-eight-card structure of Major Arcana, consisting of twenty-two archetypes, from the Fool to the World, and Minor Arcana, consisting of four suits of fourteen cards each (Wands, Pentacles, Swords, Cups), from Aces to Kings. Oracle cards offer more variety; their content and theme depend entirely upon the creator. The one I primarily used that winter had watercolor illustrations: "Redefine Boundaries," read one card; "Higher Self," read another. Whichever card I drew served a double purpose of foreshadowing how the day might take shape and giving me a shape with which to understand the events of the day. And on that day in 2013, I could see with what some call clairvoyance.

But the day went on, and the strange ability left me incrementally as though a heavy curtain were dropping, until when I closed my eyes there was only darkness. If I close my eyes right now, I still see only this ordinary darkness.

At first I mentioned this only to C., and then to one or two of my closest friends. I joked with them that as far as superhuman abilities go, being able to see what's in front of me with my eyes closed is a rather pathetic one. I certainly couldn't take that show on the road. And my "sight without sight" happened only one other time, on September 29, 2014, when I was not psychotic: again, I realized that I could see the world with my eyes closed. Again, I tested myself with colored pens and found myself to be accurate. I asked a new friend, a mystic, for advice, and she told me to contemplate whatever seemed unclear to me at the time.

My response:

> So after a bunch of fleeting images—a girl clutching a book to her chest and plummeting into the ocean—sinking for a really long time, hair floating—hits the bottom and then ricochets back up to the surface, gasping, still clutching the book, in the

middle of nowhere—looking around—a buoy appears and she struggles to climb onto it—she climbs onto it, drops the book, grabs it—sits on the buoy for a long time—the buoy eventually crashes against an island & she climbs onto the island, which is basically a large, pointy mound—when she reaches the top, the book explodes out of her arms as a white bird and flies upward—the bird goes up for a really long time (at this point I wasn't sure how it was going to go, because it felt like the bird was just going to keep going up forever)—eventually it explodes into a white light that spreads over the entire sky, enveloping the universe.

The curtain dropped again a few hours later. I haven't experienced the ability since.

If you're curious as to whether your unusual experiences are signs of mental illness or psychic ability, the internet is happy to offer an opinion. Forums dedicated to mental health in general and schizophrenia in particular are full of threads with headings such as "Have you noticed psychic ability since you became schizophrenic?," "Schizophrenia or a medium?," "Am I psychic or am I a crazy schizophrenic?," and "Psychosis and psychic powers?" Some assume that psychosis and psychic ability are mutually exclusive, while others assume that they are indeed suffering from a psychotic disorder but might also be gifted with supernatural ability. Both are potential ways to look at the silver lining of a disorder that few would see as having benefits at all.

What makes psychosis a condition that seems open to interpretation as an ability rather than an illness? For one, many psychiatric diagnoses hinge on "distress" as a criterion—it's possible to show up at a clinician's office with the hallmark symptoms of depression, but if you're not distressed, your condition won't meet the criteria for major depressive disorder. Schizophrenia is one diagnosis that doesn't require the presence of distress in addition to other symptoms, which leaves room for interpretation; without distress, a symptom might be a welcome attribute, and therefore an ability.

In *Legion*, a 2017 show based on a Marvel comic, David Haller is a man with schizophrenia, though the advertisements tantalizingly suggest he "may be more than human." The show posits that though David is institutionalized in the Clockworks Psychiatric Hospital, his symptoms are not signs of pathology but rather of supernatural gifts. The one-line description of episode one on the FX website reads, "David considers whether the voices he hears might be real." Because this is a story set in the Marvel universe, we can assume without watching that the answer to this question is "yes." As with *A Beautiful Mind*, the viewer is forced to experience reality as bewilderingly as David does. The *New Yorker*'s Emily Nussbaum reports on the show's surreal visuals, adding that "this gemstone surreality turns everything into theatre; it also forces us, like David, to absorb what we see without knowing if we can trust our perceptions." Later in the article she indicates that *Legion* is "one of those shows that treat mental illness . . . as a metaphor for being special, so if you have a problem with that approach it will not be your jam." In Twitter conversations about the show, viewers wonder if the lunacy-as-superpower narrative is, in fact, harmful to the cause of mental health advocacy, causing deluded individuals to eschew help for the sake of believing in their own magical capabilities—but such beliefs can handily thrive without the help of an FX television show.

When I began to hallucinate, in 2005—first hearing a voice, and then seeing what wasn't there—my mother suggested that these symptoms might not be pathologies but rather spiritual gifts. According to Chinese superstition, initial hallucinatory experiences may be indications that one is meant to become a "soul reader," a skill akin to a fortune-teller or medium. "People use it as a career," she told me, "so don't be scared." No one else had tried to give me a perspective on my symptoms beyond that of mental illness.

Over the next decade, I would occasionally consider the utility of seeing psychosis as an ability: I could improve my mental health by thinking of schizoaffective disorder as a tool to access something useful, as opposed to a terrifying pathology. As Viktor Frankl says in *Man's Search for Meaning*, we want our suffering, if it must be endured, to mean something. Yet I had no idea what this belief would look like in practice.

My friend Paige and I first met in 2014 through a mutual friend. She is a gregarious introvert, and in possession of a magnificent, snorting laugh. Her waist-length hair is often in Pippi Longstocking braids. She unironically describes herself as a "pizza-loving witch," and provides mystical services ranging from Tarot card reading to mediumship to shamanic journeying. For years she would come over every Tuesday to cowork with me. More than once she'd delay the work we'd intended to do with a story, say, about helping a murdered little girl—whose spirit was unhappily attached to Paige's Tenderloin apartment—cross over. I remain open to such stories because I don't believe that she would invent them. She aligns her beliefs with the Picasso quote "Everything you can imagine is real."

I was also introduced to J., an artist with occultist tendencies and a weakness for Chanel. I have yet to meet her in person, but we speak on the phone at times; I turn up the volume to catch her wispy voice through my earbuds. She once described the experience of going to Italy for the first time. She was overwhelmed, she told me, by the sounds she heard from centuries of Italian life, including a cacophony of ancient voices in fluent Italian.

In my friendships with these women, I have tried to imagine whether a psychiatrist would be comfortable venturing a diagnosis based on their seemingly logical sensory experiences—particularly sensory experiences that sound like magic. J.'s Italian recollections remind me of lucid dreams I've had in which I moved through crowds and could distinctly see every individual face. While inside the dream, I marveled at my brain's ability to hold so many faces, all of them strange, and wondered if they were invented or dredged up from memory. Although both struggle with recurrent depression, neither Paige nor J. has ever been diagnosed with a psychotic disorder, including anything in the realm of the schizophrenias.

It was Paige who introduced me to their shared spiritual mentor, Briana (Bri) Saussy, who runs a thriving online business under her own name with the tagline "Sacred arts for the soulful seeker." Education in what might be called witchcraft or occultism—what Bri dubs "the sacred arts"—frequently lacks rigor. This is not so with Bri, who graduated with both a BA and an MA in classics, the history of mathematics and science, and philosophy from St. John's College, and who cares about maintaining the strength of pedagogy alongside a life of prayer and blessing. Bri became, and still is, my spiritual mentor as well—one with whom I have had monthly calls and exchanged regular emails. In seeking her out, I was intrigued by the idea of finding a way to make sense of my idiosyncrasies and anxieties. When I mentioned this to Bri, she laughed and said, "I'm sorry to tell you this, but belief does not simplify life."

My first phone conversation with Bri was a paid consultation. I told her about being diagnosed with schizoaffective disorder and my later diagnosis of late-stage Lyme disease. After she prodded me about my dream life, I went on to tell her about my history of lucid dreaming, current issues with nightmares and PTSD, seemingly psychic experiences, hallucinations, and delusions.

She said, "It's very interesting to me that you started feeling like you were dead—and, if I understood the timing of that correctly, that sensation was happening around the onset of your Lyme disease. When I hear that, [it sounds like] it could be part of a paranoid delusion, but you *did* have a chronic illness in your body, and it was one you weren't aware of. I see that as maybe a really dramatic way of your ensouled part telling the rest of you, 'Hey, there's a problem here.'" Bri pointed to my unusual experiences as indications of being "necessarily liminal." A term she frequently uses is "thin-skinned." As she explains it, people who are thin-skinned have perceptions that are wide-open; they perceive what is happening in the other realm. Thin-skinned, or skinless, individuals will start to think they're crazy because they see, sense, and feel things outside of the regular scope of experience.

This perception of otherworldly experience is echoed in the book *Living in the Borderland: The Evolution of Consciousness and the Challenge of Healing Trauma*, by Jungian analyst Jerome S. Bernstein. Bernstein posits the idea of "Borderland personalities"—people whose sensitivities and unusual perceptions are "nothing short of sacred." "Problems result," he writes, "from the fact that most often Borderland personalities themselves do not register their own experiences as real. They have been conditioned, like the rest of us with a [W]estern ego, to identify with the negative bias against the nonrational realm of phenomenology. Thus they see their own Borderland experiences as 'crazy'—as pathological. And because they do, they become even more neurotic than would otherwise be the case."

During my first call with Bri, she recommended that I try her three-day, self-paced audio-and-workbook course about working with liminality. There was nothing about her matter-of-fact, gentle way of speaking that alarmed me, though I knew the course would cost more money than I'd already paid for the consultation. I didn't feel as though I were speaking to a charlatan—if she were, she would be of the sort who truly believed in her own trickery.

The class description for Beyond the Hedge: Foundational Techniques for Embracing the Liminal explains the titular phrase as follows: "In older times one way of talking about someone who could travel into the liminal realms was to say that they went 'beyond the hedge,' an old idiom meaning that they could travel beyond what was safe and known into territory that held mystery, magic, and great promise." The course covers three foundational techniques: using the body's intuition, working with talismanic cords, and building relationships with allies and spirit guides.

Exploring the possibilities of the sacred arts brought up the question of medication. Even as I considered that I might be thin-skinned, and therefore privy to otherworldly experiences, at no point was I inclined to quit talk therapy or my regimen of psychopharmacological drugs. Perhaps this seems contradictory, or indicative of skepticism, but I knew that I'd suffered greatly during psychosis and was not interested in turning face-first, again, into the storm of bleak and blustering insanity. By learning about the liminal, I was not trying to prolong my psychotic experiences, but attempting to make sense of them. I wanted to create a container for what had happened to me and shove the nastiness in.

The second-century Gnostics claimed that among ordinary Christians lived the *pneumatikoi*, elite believers who possessed spiritual wisdom beyond that of their peers. The *pneumatikoi* could speak in tongues—a phenomenon called glossolalia—as evidence of being possessed by the Spirit; though occasionally intelligible, glossolalia "for the most part . . . consisted of frenzied, inarticulate, incoherent, ecstatic speech." The psychiatric term for inarticulate, babbling speech is "schizophasia," or "word salad," and it is one of the more visible symptoms of schizophrenia. Incoherent speech may indicate truths too profound to be understood by the lowly; it may also indicate a deterioration of the mind.

Language was central to Jacques Lacan's distinction between illness and mysticism. He compared the writings of Daniel Schreber, a judge and famous sufferer of what was then called "dementia praecox," to those of John of the Cross, stating that, as John Gale writes, "while John of the Cross wrote in a poetic way, Schreber did not." The former's poeticism opens spiritual dimensions for the reader, where the latter's babbling shuts them down.

The line between insanity and mysticism is thin; the line between reality and unreality is thin. Liminality as a spiritual concept is all about the porousness of boundaries. "Liminal" and "medial"— the latter a term most associated with "the Medial Woman," as conceived of by Swiss Jungian analyst Toni Wolff—are often used interchangeably, and refer to the gray area between here and the otherworld. In Beyond the Hedge, Bri describes the otherworld in metaphors: "the realms above" and "the realms below" Earth, "middle Earth," "fairyland," or "imaginal realms." Death is the only manifestation of the otherworld that I can understand; birth and death are obvious manifestations of the liminal. To a lesser extent, I've considered the otherworld through major illness, trauma, and marriage, which are also liminal conditions, and, unlike dying, have marked and scarred the timeline of my life.

The metaphor-laden otherworld is accompanied by a metaphor-laden liminal space. Clarissa Pinkola Estés, PhD, a scholar, poet, and the author of *Women Who Run with the Wolves: Myths and Stories of the Wild Woman Archetype*, describes a mythological old woman who "stands between the worlds of rationality and mythos. . . . This land between the worlds is that inexplicable place we all recognize once we experience it, but its nuances slip away and shape-change if one tries to pin them down." The liminal can also be described in psychoanalytic lingo; Estés refers to "the locus betwixt the worlds," referring to Jung's concept of "the collective unconscious, the [objective] psyche, and the psychoid unconscious." Estés goes on to say that this locus, "the crack between the worlds—is the place where visitations, miracles, imaginations, inspirations, and healings of all natures occur." Fairyland may seem quite different from the collective unconscious, but this is Bri's point in coining the phrase "sacred arts": she aims to credit the variety of faiths and traditions that feed her practice. In Beyond the Hedge, she explains that liminal work crosses different faiths and religions, and those faiths and religions have, in turn, developed individual ways to journey into the otherworld, and individuals often return bearing gifts for the community.

And yet liminal experiences, as Bri describes them, are not necessarily unusual or gifted to a special few. Dreams are the most common expression of liminality—more common than, say, seeing or feeling the presence of saints, angels, or God, which are all liminal experiences. To work with the liminal is to probe the notion of what is real versus imaginary, or even psychotic. In the beginning of Bri's Beyond the Hedge workbook, she writes, "Anyone who wishes to gain proficiency in liminal work is going to have to become comfortable with the unseen. One of the best expressions of this are the words of Jesus Christ to St. Thomas: 'Blessed are they who did not see, and yet believed.'" Working with the liminal involves working with faith. One article of faith is *This suffering will be of use to you someday.*

Bri says it this way: "I think that when we're talking about . . . schizophrenia, we really want to be clear about what is rational, two plus two equals four; what is irrational, two plus two equals spaghetti sauce; and what is nonrational. . . . A lot of people who are diagnosed with schizophrenia that I have spoken with, that I have worked with . . . are not irrational at all." The divine is nonrational and indicates the limits of symbolic understanding; insanity is irrational and indicates a structural failure of reality.

The nonrational psychotics, Bri tells me, have intact reasoning, "but it's coming, or it's partially informed, I would say is usually the case, from a different source than what we're used to. There's an internal logic, and often their insights are dead-on if you can peel back the code that those insights are often delivered in, and start to understand how that internal logic works." She judges psychosis by its utility: "If there's something of use there, then you take it. And so even if it's a scary vision, if there's something of use there that you can take and you can apply to your life, I wouldn't consider that schizophrenic. I would consider that liminal."

Our world values what is rational, and fears what is irrational: the raving homeless man on the morning bus; the murderous, delusional "psychos" we see on *Law & Order*—*law and order* being, after all, the ultimate institutions of rationality and reason. To understand the nonrational takes looking beyond the surface, and is the realm of the mystical.

Recall that I experienced my first hallucination in my early twenties as a senior at Stanford, and had been diagnosed with bipolar disorder at the age of eighteen. The voice in the dorm shower had said, quite clearly, "I hate you." What amazes me about hallucinations is the efficacy with which they kidnap the senses. The voice that said it hated me was as real as any other sound in that room. I in fact wondered if I was subject to a phenomenon having to do with the drain and the pipe system—perhaps I was hearing something said on another floor, and yet upon consideration, the voice didn't seem to be coming from the ground.

I finished my shower, dried off, and returned to my dorm room wrapped in a towel. I told my roommate, who was aware, albeit abstractly, of my mental health issues, that I'd heard a voice in the shower. I was stunned by what had happened, but was calm as I recounted the story.

"You're *crazy*," she said.

But what if the voice held some sort of function? I can reach for interpretations—the most obvious one being that I did hate myself at the time, which had fed self-destructive behaviors for years. Perhaps the voice was saying that if I didn't find a better therapist, my self-destructiveness would eventually sink me in grave danger. This message strikes me as too basic to be worthy of a hallucination, but then again, who am I to judge?

I listened to the three Beyond the Hedge MP3s in bed, one per day, flipping through the accompanying PDF on my iPad while I listened. Bri lectures by phone in the recordings; the class was initially taught over the phone with live participants, who then asked questions when the line was opened for questioning.

What I have found most useful from Bri's teachings is the use of talismanic cords. Bri gives a few uses for such cords during liminal work. According to her, the cord offers protection depending on where it's tied: a cord around the stomach reins in desire, while one tied around the head prevents overthinking. I anointed a linen ribbon of unknown provenance with an oil Bri had mailed to me, labeled Balm of Gilead. I tie the ribbon around my ankle when I begin to feel as though I'm slipping. I'm not like Paige, who uses a cord before actively journeying into the otherworld. Though it seems antithetical to the point of the course, I don't *want* to go into the liminal realms. I want to know how to control myself when frightening things happen to me, and if there's a chance that a ribbon around my ankle will keep me either tethered to this world or safer, somehow, when I do tumble out of it—though it may need to be used in tandem with medication, and reported to my psychiatrist—that's good enough for me.

After all, the otherworld was not made to be visited too cavalierly by mere mortals. In *Women Who Run with the Wolves*, Estés uses the story of Vasalisa and the Baba Yaga to caution against dithering in other realms. At one point in the story, the Baba Yaga tries to tempt Vasalisa into asking too many questions about the oddities of the Baba Yaga's world, but the wise doll in Vasalisa's pocket jumps up and down, warning her to stop. This, Estés says, is a caution against "calling upon too much of the numinosity of the underworld all at once . . . for though we visit there, we do not want to become enraptured and thereby trapped there."

I met Bri in person at the Downtown Subscription café in Santa Fe one winter, during my nine-day trip for Lyme treatment. Porochista and I had been shuttling from place to place, and my arms were bruised and dotted with marks from various IVs by the time I arrived. Bri was already there, waiting with tea; we greeted each other with hugs and exclamations. I sat on the tall chair across from her, concerned about how long my body would be able to hold itself up so far off the ground, and I was already exhausted—the day had been a hard one, as Porochista had learned that morning of her longtime friend's suicide. Travis had been announced missing the day before. That morning, Porochista had said, "I think he's alive. I think he just . . . went off somewhere." I looked over at her a few hours later. She was sitting on the bed, hunched over her phone and crying.

For Bri and me to be meeting in person at all was something of a miracle—when I settled in and asked her whether work had brought her to Santa Fe, she said that she'd driven the thirteen hours from

San Antonio with her husband and son just to see me. I smiled. Dear God, please help me, I thought, struggling to remain upright. I told her about what had happened to Porochista. I asked if there was anything we should do.

"What I do when anyone dies," she said, "is to go and light a candle for them. I would go to the Our Lady of Guadalupe shrine in town and I would light a candle for them. The other thing that I think is important to understand after death happens is that a lot of traditions say that there's a three-day period where the line is a little staticy as they're sort of adjusting. But blessing [Travis], and blessing his family, is a good thing to start doing now, as well as being open to signs and omens of him communicating with her directly. A song might come on that she associates with him, or words on a sign, words on a magazine."

As she spoke, I noticed the abundance of *milagro* heart charms, or folk amulets, in Bri's jewelry and about her person. Later that week, on a journey to Chimayó, I would see similar *milagros* for sale in the gift shops; I bought a red wooden cross adorned with *milagros* that now hangs above my altar. Bri's eyelids and rosy cheeks shimmered with gold dust. I told her about what had happened to Porochista, who had accompanied me to the café and was sitting across the room. "Ageless," Porochista called her, once we were back in our motel room.

Bri and I chatted about magic and its utility during oppressive political times (Donald Trump was to be inaugurated later that month); the new *Star Wars* movie, *Rogue One*; the importance of work ("Whatever your work is, that work matters. It's about touching the people that you're here to touch in the best possible way"); her route from lawyer-to-be to teaching the sacred arts online; the origin of the sacred arts in her life. A terrific thing about conversing with a teacher, particularly when ill, is that there's no need to carry the conversation—give a good prompt or question, and they'll happily expound. But I wrapped up the conversation after about an hour, feeling guilty for having brought her so far to chat with me for such a short time. Still, I felt no judgment from her. "You seem tired," she said. "Please, go rest."

Instead of going straight back to our motel, which we knew would lead to an unbreakable inertia, Porochista and I made our way to the Our Lady of Guadalupe shrine. The sun had set, taking any wintry warmth with it. We moved slowly because Porochista was using a cane, and the ground was covered with hazardous patches of black ice. We had no candle to light, but there were clear boxes filled with petitions, and I told her that she could write a message to tuck into one of the boxes. I waited on an ice-cold bench and stared at the Lady's benevolent, smooth face. For the Guadalupe Feast Day the previous month, Bri had sent out a prayer that included these words: "Wherever there is loss, sadness, gaping holes full of the howling winds of grief and sorrow—there She is." We'd gone to the shrine for Porochista's friend, yes, but also, and perhaps mainly, for Porochista and her grief.

I originally went to Bri because psychosis had made me fear my own mind. Since then, the sacred arts have given me some solace not so much through the beliefs they provide as through the actions they recommend. To say this prayer—burn this candle—perform this ritual—create this salt or honey jar—is to have something to do when it seems that nothing can be done.

At the time of this writing, I haven't experienced a hallucination in years. There occur a few visual blips, or occasionally a loud clap in the room when no one's there, but my senses have otherwise been absent of maggot-ridden corpses or eerie voices. My last serious episode of delusional thinking is four years behind me. But there are the episodes that foretell psychosis, or even mild psychosis—the episodes in which I must tread carefully to keep myself where I am. When a certain kind of psychic detachment occurs, I retrieve my ribbon; I tie it around my ankle. I tell myself that should delusion come to call, or hallucinations crowd my senses again, I might be able to wrangle sense out of the senseless. I tell myself that if I must live with a slippery mind, I want to know how to tether it too.

Acknowledgments

The Collected Schizophrenias could not have happened without the assistance of many people and organizations, and I would like to express gratitude for those people and organizations here.

For my best reader and dear friend, who helped to shape the essays inside this book, Miriam Lawrence. Your advice and love have been invaluable to me. For Andi Winnette, who jumped right in when this book needing the jumping. Thank you for your brilliance. Thank you to Quince Mountain for going through the manuscript with me in the home stretch—you are one of the wisest people I know.

For the encouragement, friendship, and unwavering support of Anna North, Laura Turner, Caille Millner, Reese Kwon, Andi and Colin Winnette, Anisse Gross, Dyana Valentine, Rachel Khong, Porochista Khakpour, and Aaron Silberstein. For the everyday cheerleading of the SDC: thank you.

For the editors with whom I worked on several of these essays, including Andi Winnette, Karolina Waclawiak, Mensah Demary,

Anna North, Willie Osterweil, Haley Cullingham, and Bethany Rose Lamont. For Nicole Cliffe, who was the first person to enthusiastically accept one of these essays for publication—it took a while for "Perdition Days" to find its home, and I'm thankful that it was with you.

For my healing team.

For Hedgebrook, The Corporation of Yaddo, the Whiting Foundation, and *Granta*.

For Lana Del Rey and the album *Ultraviolence*.

For the researchers, authors, and scientists whose work I refer to in these pages, and for the people who generously allowed me to interview them for this book. For the Mental Health Association of San Francisco.

For my incredible agent and advocate, Jin Auh, and to the Wylie Agency as a whole.

For my savvy, kind editor Steve Woodward, as well as Ethan Nosowsky, Fiona McCrae, and the rest of the pack at Graywolf Press, who embraced this book and its author with enthusiasm. Special thanks to Brigid Hughes, who selected my manuscript for the Graywolf Press Nonfiction Prize: I am humbled by this astonishing opportunity.

For my family: Mom, Dad, Allen, Claudia, and Kerrigan.

For the beautiful family that I married into.

For Daphne.

Finally, for Chris, my dearest darling, to whom this book is dedicated, and who has been there for me in too many ways to recount. I love you.

ESMÉ WEIJUN WANG is the author of *The Border of Paradise*, named one of NPR's Best Books of 2016. Her essays and stories have appeared in *Catapult, Elle,* and the *Believer,* among other publications. She received the Whiting Award in 2018 and was named one of *Granta's* Best of Young American Novelists in 2017. Her other awards include the Hopwood Award for a novel-in-progress, the Louis Sudler Prize in the Performing and Creative Arts in the field of creative writing from Stanford University, and a grant from the Elizabeth George Foundation. She holds an MFA from the University of Michigan and lives in San Francisco.

The Graywolf Press Nonfiction Prize

The Collected Schizophrenias by Esmé Weijun Wang is the 2016 winner of the Graywolf Press Nonfiction Prize. Graywolf awards this prize to a previously unpublished, full-length work of outstanding literary nonfiction by a writer who is not yet established in the genre. Previous winners include *Riverine: A Memoir from Anywhere but Here* by Angela Palm, *Leaving Orbit: Notes from the Last Days of American Spaceflight* by Margaret Lazarus Dean, *The Empathy Exams: Essays* by Leslie Jamison, *The Grey Album: On the Blackness of Blackness* by Kevin Young, *Notes from No Man's Land: American Essays* by Eula Biss, *Black Glasses Like Clark Kent: A GI's Secret from Postwar Japan* by Terese Svoboda, *Neck Deep and Other Predicaments* by Ander Monson, and *Frantic Transmissions to and from Los Angeles: An Accidental Memoir* by Kate Braverman.

The Graywolf Press Nonfiction Prize seeks to acknowledge—and honor—the great traditions of literary nonfiction. Whether grounded in observation, autobiography, or research, much of the most beautiful, daring, and original writing over the past few decades can be categorized as nonfiction.

The 2016 prize judge was Brigid Hughes, founding editor of *A Public Space*.

The Graywolf Press Nonfiction Prize is funded in part by endowed gifts from the Arsham Ohanessian Charitable Remainder Unitrust and the Ruth Easton Fund of the Edelstein Family Foundation.

Arsham Ohanessian, an Armenian born in Iraq who came to the United States in 1952, was an avid reader and a tireless advocate for human rights and peace. He strongly believed in the power of literature and education to make a positive impact on humanity.

Ruth Easton, born in North Branch, Minnesota, was a Broadway actress in the 1920s and 1930s. The Ruth Easton Fund of the Edelstein Family Foundation is pleased to support the work of emerging artists and writers in her honor.

Graywolf Press is grateful to Arsham Ohanessian and Ruth Easton for their generous support.

The text of *The Collected Schizophrenias*
is set in Adobe Jenson Pro.
Book design by Rachel Holscher.
Composition by Bookmobile Design and Digital
Publisher Services, Minneapolis, Minnesota.
Manufactured by Versa Press on acid-free,
30 percent postconsumer wastepaper.